Cramm
This
Book

Cramm This Book

So You Know WTF Is Going On in the World Today

Olivia Seltzer

PHILOMEL BOOKS

An imprint of Penguin Random House LLC, New York

First published in the United States of America by Philomel Books,
an imprint of Penguin Random House LLC, 2022

Philomel Books is a registered trademark of Penguin Random House LLC.

Visit us online at penguinrandomhouse.com.

Library of Congress Cataloging-in-Publication Data is available.

Printed in the USA

ISBN 9780593352168

1 3 5 7 9 10 8 6 4 2

LSCC

Edited by Talia Benamy

Design by Monique Sterling

Text set in Aptifer Slab LT Pro

This is a work of nonfiction. Some names and identifying details have been changed.

CONTENTS

The Disasters

Cramm This Intro

I was twelve years old when I decided I needed to change the world.

Or maybe *decided* isn't the right word. It wasn't like I woke up one day and just went, "There are a lot of problems in the world. I should probably do something." No, there was a greater shift taking place.

It was the shift from feeling safe and secure within my country . . . to feeling both the absolute and urgent need to *do something* and the utter helplessness that comes with believing you're too young and your voice is too small to do much of anything. That shift happened with the 2016 US presidential election.

I'll be honest: before that election, politics rarely crossed my mind. I watched the news each night with my parents, and I certainly had big opinions about a lot of what was going on, but I never saw myself as being directly impacted by anything I watched. And I know I wasn't alone in that feeling.

Like so many of my peers, I had been part of the American school system since kindergarten, and thus I had been raised on the idea that the United States of America was simply *better*. We brought democracy to the world, we fought for the freedom of our people and others, we were economically and politically superior, we were a melting pot of immigrants from all over the planet, and so on. This was the world that I saw and the world that I was taught about, and from my position of relative privilege, it all made perfect sense.

I was raised Jewish, the great-granddaughter of family who were forced to flee the Soviet Union in the 1930s due to the pogroms—mass killing of Jews—and who eventually made their way as immigrants to Mexico, and then finally the US. So I knew that antisemitism was real, but I had never experienced it directly, or even had awareness that it was a problem that continued to exist in America. Along with many other Americans, I believed it had been vanquished with the Nazis. I knew of the Ku Klux Klan and neo-Nazi groups, but I was convinced that these were isolated cases, extremists who had no real influence on society. I was white, I was comfortable, and while I knew that our country and our world had some problems, I also had never really experienced them up close and personal.

In 2016, everything changed.

I'll set the scene. It was the day after the election, and everyone was in a bit of a daze. The majority of the students at my junior high school were Latinx, and many of their parents were undocumented immigrants.

For the first time in my life, I saw how what was happening in our government was deeply personal to me and everyone else at my school. If you weren't the child of an undocumented immigrant, you knew someone who was or were friends with someone who did. The whispered conversations about what would happen if somebody's mother or father was deported were unavoidable. The fear hung heavy in the air for weeks following the election.

It was all we could talk about.

Around the same time, my parents sat down with my younger brother and me to discuss recent reports of antisemitic acts in the United States. One such act was the spray-painting of swastikas and antisemitic language in a New York subway station. The image of a graffitied *Jews belong in the oven* was forever imprinted in my mind.

Which brings me to that overwhelming sense of helplessness I mentioned earlier. I had quickly but forcefully grown deeply disillusioned, and I was desperate to do something—*anything*—to make things right.

But for all that desperation, I truly had no idea where to start. And not just that—I had no idea how to even *think about* where to start. I was twelve years old, far too young to vote or get involved with an existing organization in any meaningful way. I felt entirely locked out of conventional systems of changemaking.

I dealt with this frustration by having long conversations with my friends about the news and politics. And that's when I noticed something: while my generation was talking about these things, none of us were really reading or watching any form of traditional news. It wasn't hard to understand why: traditional media is primarily created by older generations who just don't have younger readers in mind when writing the news. Try *watching* the news and you'll see ads for things like fighting hair loss—not really an issue for Generation Z.

I immediately identified this as a huge problem. Every day, something happens in the world that impacts countless lives. And if we don't know about these things, we're doing a serious disservice to the people who most need our help.

I knew what I had to do. One evening in January of 2017, I locked myself in a room at home and spent the next few hours researching the news and rewriting it in a way that spoke to Generation Z.

A week later, I bought the domain name thecramm.com with money from my thirteenth birthday. (The name "The Cramm" came from cramming the news into one newsletter and also referenced how students cram the night before a test—but with The Cramm, they wouldn't need to cram for the news.) A week after that, I hit send on the first of what became hundreds of newsletters detailing the news of the day in language that was engaging and digestible and, most importantly, connected to my generation.

The reaction was beyond my wildest hopes and dreams. Our newsletters, which we now send out through our website, email, text, social media, and a podcast, rake up millions of views each month. Our readers hail from over one hundred countries on six continents. I constantly receive emails from Gen Zers who tell me that something they read in The Cramm inspired them to take action and make a difference. Our readers are organizing marches and rallies, creating clubs, getting involved in charities, voting, raising awareness about the issues that matter, talking about politics with their friends—the list goes on.

As I spent more and more time distilling the news into a five-minute read, I began to recognize more and more problems with traditional media. High among them is the belief that most—if not all—of the consumers of any given news source are of an older generation that has perhaps lived through certain events that my generation has not. This leads to an expectation that anyone reading or tuning in has existing knowledge of certain issues, events, and topics, simply based on having lived through them.

While that might not be an issue for older generations, my generation, for the most part, lacks this existing knowledge, and I was constantly having to do extra research on events that had taken place years earlier just to get through a story on something happening today.

But of course, most everything that goes on in our news and politics today is tied to history. It's hard to get a grasp on the hardships marginalized people/groups face in everyday life without understanding the complex ways in which issues like racism and homophobia have manifested over time. It's hard to get a grasp on the current relationship between the US and Russia without understanding the Cold War. It's hard to get a grasp on the current situation in the Middle East without understanding the Arab Spring revolutions or the history of the Israel-Palestine conflict. It's hard to get a grasp on the Black Lives Matter movement without understanding the civil rights movement and all that it accomplished—and all that has yet to be accomplished. And it's hard to get a grasp on the future of climate change without understanding how it not only is devastating the world today through things like wildfires and hurricanes, but has also been doing damage for decades.

Understanding these events and issues is crucial to understanding the world as it is today.

So, once again, I found myself doing the very same thing I did in 2017: I locked myself in my room. I opened my computer.

And I began to type.

The result is this book, which I hope forces you to reckon with not only the state of our world today, but also how and why it came to be this way. I hope it empowers you and inspires you to take the future into your own hands.

And, above all, I hope it gives you the insight you need to ensure that history doesn't repeat itself—and to dismantle or improve the systems that have allowed so many of our worst prejudices to continue to thrive and to impact the forces that have caused such devastation to occur.

Because, after all: you can't change the world unless you know about it.

THE ISMS AND

THE PHOBIAS

Maybe you experience them on the street. Maybe you feel their effect hovering over every decision you make, enveloping every word, every action directed toward you. Maybe you see people you know having to deal with them. Even if you don't, you probably learn about them in history class in school, or talk about them with your friends.

Whatever your story is . . . you've probably had some sort of experience with the isms and phobias of the world.

Xenophobia. Sexism. Racism. Nationalism. Homophobia, transphobia, biphobia. Ableism. Islamophobia. Antisemitism.

It's no secret that these ten prejudices (and, unfortunately, so many more) pretty much rule our world. And—surprise, surprise—they rule our politics and our history, too. But it's not all that often that we take a second to actually break down what these isms and phobias mean, where they come from, and just how deeply they impact our way of life.

Before I get into that, there are a few key things to understand. Specifically, how these isms and phobias latched on to our world . . . and continue to infect it, even in this very instant. It all comes down to a single word: power.

That's right. Every single ism and phobia has to do with power. In particular: an imbalance of power. And when there's an imbalance of power, it really means that the people kept up by the system in place have direct power over the people kept down. Sexism? Keeps women down—and men up. Racism? Keeps people of color down—and white people up. Transphobia? Keeps transgender people down—and cisgender people up. I could do this all day.

That's the thing about all these isms and phobias. They exist to keep systems of power in place. Systems of unfair, unjust power that pretty much serve only a very particular group of people.

But there's a flip side to that. Through the actions you take, the words you use, the choices you make, you can uphold these systems of power . . . but you can also dismantle them.

Fair warning: This book will attempt to pull back the curtain on how our world is set up, and how that structure came to be. These isms and phobias are a huge part of that. And while it might make you uncomfortable at times, it will also reveal just how devastating an impact all these isms and phobias have, in ways you may have never even considered.

It will also empower you.

Are you ready to do what it takes to change the world?

Read on.

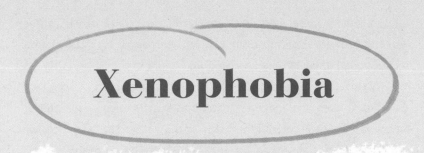

Xenophobia

Xenophobia (noun): **dislike of or prejudice against people from other countries or those perceived to be foreign**

The Holocaust. The murder of Black people by the Ku Klux Klan. Nineteenth- and twentieth-century human zoos. Japanese American incarceration camps in the US in the 1940s, and Uighur Muslim internment camps in China in the twenty-first century. Colonists' brutalization of Native Americans. Anti-Asian sentiment during the coronavirus pandemic.

What do these events all have in common?

They're all acts of **xenophobia**.

Heads up: I'll be chatting about a whole lot of different isms and phobias in this section—from racism to homophobia—but xenophobia is the broadest. It's rooted less in specific characteristics and more in the general idea that anything foreign = bad. Or rather, any*one* foreign. It stems from two key elements: fear (aka latent xenophobia) and hatred (aka virulent xenophobia). And yes, this can totally turn into something like racism or Islamophobia.

But it goes even deeper than thinking someone is inferior because of, say, the color of their skin or their religion. Xenophobia is the firm belief that anyone foreign (read: different or other) doesn't belong, whether it's in a school or a workplace, a neighborhood, a city, or even a country as a whole. And some xenophobes go to extreme lengths to ensure that those they consider different never do.

Take a look at some examples of xenophobia—and yes, there's a wide range of ways it can appear in our world. But just like in this chart, it can all intensify pretty quickly as you go.

ACT	EXAMPLE
Avoiding a person from a particular place or background	Crossing the road when you see a Black person
Making "in spite of" comments	"Well, they're nice/smart/ pretty for a _____ person."
Being dismissive of or condescending toward a person from a particular place or background	"You don't know what you're talking about because you're from ____."
Being suspicious of a person from a particular place or background	Following someone around in a retail store because of the color of their skin

Fearing and disliking immigrants	"These immigrants are taking our jobs!"
Stereotyping a person from a particular place or background	"Oh, you're Asian—you must be good at school."
Telling someone to "go back where they came from"	Pretty self-explanatory
Using one bad experience to justify xenophobia	"I was bullied by a ____ person!"
Using hateful language (think: slurs) to degrade someone	That one's pretty self-explanatory, too.
Taking some sort of action against someone because they are from a particular place or background	Calling the police on someone because of what they look like, or ripping off someone's hijab
Making laws specifically designed to oppress people from a particular place or background	You'll hear more about some of these laws later, including gerrymandering, redlining, and the Muslim ban.
Blaming people from a particular place or background for your/your country's problems	"They took my spot in that college because they're ____."
Imprisoning a group of people simply because they're part of a particular group	I'll say it again: internment camps. Also: the war on drugs, which has disproportionately impacted people of color.

Expelling people from a particular location or background from a place or institution simply because they're from that location or background	ICYMI, the Bangladesh gov kicked lots of Rohingya Muslim kids out of schools in 2019.
Taking military action against a group of people based on their background, race, or ethnicity	Since 2015, Turkey's been launching a military campaign targeting Kurds, an ethnic minority there.
Working to violently eliminate a group of people	The Holocaust—plus a too-long list of other genocides

And let me reiterate: it's easier than it may seem for small, subtle acts of xenophobia to escalate into violence. Look at the origins of any genocide and you'll find the same pattern—from a quiet fear of others to not-so-quietly degrading them to openly attacking them to enacting laws to oppress them to taking extreme military action against them . . .

So, as you continue reading, be sure to keep this chart in mind. Watch out for these acts of xenophobia. And take note of how quickly the beginning can lead to the end.

Literally.

Sexism

Sexism (noun): **prejudice, stereotyping, or discrimination, typically against women, on the basis of sex**

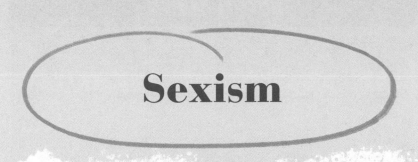

If you're a woman, chances are you've faced sexism. Maybe it looks like being objectified. Or maybe it looks like being seen as mentally or physically inferior. Hey—ever been criticized for being overly emotional? That right there is sexist. Sexism has been keeping women down for centuries, throughout the rise and fall of countless empires and govs.

Below, I lay out a whole slew of examples of how sexism can play out. Because, news flash . . . there are a lot. And they're not always all that easy to spot—especially since sometimes, sexism can come across as being chivalrous or respectful, when in actuality, it's really not.

You'll see what I mean.

HOSTILE SEXISM

"You throw like a girl!"

"You're so calculated/dramatic/bossy/emotional/aggressive/annoying."

Mansplaining, manpeating . . . you get the idea

Victim blaming ("She was sexually assaulted? Well, what was she wearing? Was she drunk?")

I'll repeat: thinking women aren't as smart or strong as men

Objectifying women, both on and off the screen, or putting unrealistic beauty standards on women

Paying women less than men for the same job or passing over a woman for a job she's qualified for just because she's, you know, a woman

"Women belong in the kitchen" or, more generally, overemphasizing the importance of getting married and having kids

Assuming a woman working in an office is a secretary instead of a CEO, or that a woman in a hospital is a nurse instead of a doctor

Designating things like toys, books, movies, and games as "for girls" and "for boys" just because of sexist stereotypes about the kinds of things girls are expected to like. Think: assuming only boys want to play with basketballs and only girls want to play with Barbie dolls, associating pink with girls and blue with boys, immediately assuming any book or movie with a female protagonist is just for girls . . . to name a few. It's only one way in which gender stereotyping starts *young*. This is on the edge between hostile and benevolent sexism, since it's not so openly sexist but totally has a damaging outcome.

"BENEVOLENT" SEXISM

Putting women on a pedestal (think: all those movies where the hero's prize is the perfect, lovely, kind princess who is practically worshiped)

The idea that women need to be protected by men because they're supposedly fragile and delicate (that whole "damsel in distress" trope)

The belief that women are more caring, nurturing, and empathetic

"I don't hit girls."

The belief that women are inherently more emotionally intelligent and intuitive

The belief that women are inherently cleaner and neater

Being called a "good girl" or names like "darling" and "sweetie." It's not necessarily sexist if it's a term of endearment from a loved one, but if it comes from some stranger on the street or your male boss, it can be pretty degrading.

Thinking a woman's love completes or fixes a man

Movies displaying any of the above. See: *The Amazing Spider-Man*, *Grease*, the Twilight saga, *Cinderella* . . . and the list goes on.

Yeah, that's all pretty sexist. And there are a gazillion more instances of sexism that didn't make this list, but are also valid.

Hostile sexism is a loooot a lot easier to identify . . . but benevolent sexism can be just as harmful. Don't believe me? Studies show that when women face benevolent sexism, they actually perform worse on working memory and cognitive resources tasks. The why: benevolent sexism causes women to think less of themselves and actually reinforces hostile sexism in a quiet, behind-the-scenes kind of way (hi, internalized misogyny). Hostile sexism has also been shown to be much more prevalent in countries with lots of benevolent sexism.

But sexism goes beyond individual people's actions and words. Sexism can be institutional (which, for the record, means pretty much the same thing as systemic in this context).

In other words: because men have had a biiiiig advantage in society since modern society was created (think: being allowed to own land, run businesses, drive cars, cast their ballot . . . to name a few), our society itself can be pretty darn sexist. All of the sexist things I mentioned in the chart above have become so ingrained in nearly every aspect of our world—from the movies we watch to the extracurricular activities we're encouraged to engage in—that they have become normalized.

They have become invisible.

Which leads them to become even more damaging.

And yes—sexism doesn't just impact women. Men can be harmed by sexist rhetoric, too.

"Stop being such a p*ssy."

Bet you've heard that before. It all stems from this overwhelming belief that men need to suppress their feelings in an attempt to act *manly* and *macho*. Men can be laughed at for crying or showing emotion. They're expected to be strong and anything but (stereotypically) feminine.

The consequences are extreme.

The majority of people who die by suicide in the US (and a number of other countries around the world) are men—even though more women report having suicidal thoughts and get diagnosed with depression. It's not hard to figure out why: men don't feel like they can or even should reach out for help, because doing so isn't seen as "manly."

Keep an eye out for sexist behavior as you move through not only this book, but the world in general. And not just the more obvious and openly sinister hostile sexism, but also the more veiled and just-as-dangerous benevolent sexism. Because once you know to look for it . . . it's impossible to avoid.

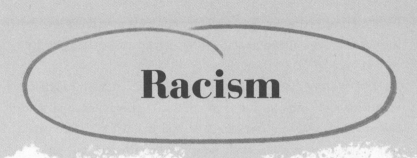

Racism

Racism (noun): prejudice, discrimination, or antagonism directed against a person or people on the basis of their membership in a particular racial or ethnic group, typically one that is a minority or marginalized

Wherever you are in the world, if you're BIPOC (which stands for Black, Indigenous, and people of color), you've probably experienced racism. Racism affects different people and groups in totally different ways, but the outcome? Well, that's never good.

Racism can take a lot of forms, so it helps to break it down into a few key categories: individual, systemic, overt, and covert. Individual racism is pretty self-explanatory—it's when individual people engage in racist behavior. Systemic? Not so much. While individual racism exists on a human-to-human basis, systemic racism comes through on a society-to-human basis. It's the gazillion ways in which our society keeps people of color oppressed.

Meanwhile, overt racism is anything that is very obviously and very clearly racist. Things can be either individually and overtly racist—like racial slurs—or systemically and overtly racist—like police brutality. Same goes for covert racism, which is anything that is more sneakily racist. It's not always intentionally racist—like the whole "I don't see color" thing, which is also individual racism—but the impact is arguably just as harmful. And there's plenty of systemic covert racism as well. Case in point: whitewashing education, forced assimilation . . . the list goes on.

Oh, wait. It literally does.

Let's take a look at some racism-related terms, tropes, and systems that tend to—unfortunately—pop up a lot.

TOKENISM: Ever heard of performative activism? That's when a person talks the talk, but doesn't walk the walk when it comes to activism—like all those people who post angrily on Instagram every time another act of police brutality occurs . . . but don't do much else. And ICYDK, it goes hand in hand with tokenism, which is when a person or group makes a symbolic attempt at being inclusive, usually for the sake of appearances. This often plays out when companies or organizations do the bare minimum with hiring people of color, just to make it seem like they're being diverse and inclusive. Not good, since it uses people of color for commercial gain without actually trying to fix issues of racism in the workplace.

WHITE SAVIOR COMPLEX: Aka when white people try to "rescue" nonwhite people. It might seem positive, but lots of times, it leads to the mic being taken away from people of color and white voices being centered instead in conversations or stories about people of color. It can also be pretty darn patronizing. This one is related to performative activism, too, and it's a very, very common trope in media. (Think: *The Help*; *The Blind Side*; *McFarland, USA* . . . to name a few.)

TONE POLICING: When someone who is part of a minority or marginalized group gets flak for the emotion with which they deliver their message, totally taking away from the message itself. "You need to calm down." Tone policing. "You're being too emotional." Tone policing. "Stop being so angry." Yep, that's tone policing, too.

"I DON'T SEE COLOR" OR "THERE'S ONLY ONE HUMAN RACE": Sure, in theory, this is meant to invalidate racists. Buuuut it actually ends up invalidating people of color and the hardships they face by ignoring the fact that they go through vastly different experiences from white people due to the color of their skin. And you can't exactly fix a problem if the problem's not being acknowledged in the first place. It also ignores the fact that different races and ethnicities might have specific traditions or elements of heritage that should be celebrated, rather than erased under the banner of one shared humanity.

"YOU DON'T SOUND_____ " (WHERE THAT BLANK IS FILLED IN BY THE RACE OF THE PERSON IN QUESTION) OR *"YOU'RE SO ARTICULATE":* (a) There's lots of stereotyping and generalizing going on here, since there's an underlying assumption that all people of a certain race sound similar, and (b) telling someone they're articulate pretty much lets them know you didn't expect them to be, and you're surprised to hear they actually are.

REDLINING: When an institution shakes its head at offering someone some sort of service (like banking or healthcare) just because the person lives in a certain area. It originated during the era of segregation in the twentieth century as a way to keep majority-BIPOC neighborhoods locked out of these services, and it's technically illegal. Only one slight problem . . . it's still taking place across the US.

GERRYMANDERING: When a state unfairly draws district lines to favor a certain political party in elections. It can also be used to stifle the voices of people of color and minimize the impact of their votes.

WHITEWASHING: Taking one big eraser to BIPOC history, music, art, and culture to center white people and their experiences, or crediting white people for the accomplishments of BIPOC. For many of us in the US, in school, it manifests as sugarcoated versions of history (especially when it comes to slavery and the treatment of Native Americans) that leave white people coming out looking better. In other words: more innocent.

MODEL MINORITY MYTH: The idea that anyone who is part of a particular minority group is more successful than others around them. (This is often something we see ascribed to people of Asian cultures.) In school, this often plays out with stereotypes of the *perfect student*—works extra hard, gets good grades, is maybe pressured by an immigrant parent or a "tiger mom," and could even be a musical genius. Not good, since it generalizes an entire group of people who are actually very diverse, holds people from that group to a different standard, and *others* people from that group. You know, makes them seem like foreigners, or outsiders. It can also harm other marginalized groups by serving as a comparison to the "right" way to succeed as a person of color.

BLACKFACE, BROWNFACE, YELLOWFACE: Putting on makeup or otherwise altering your appearance in an attempt to make yourself look like you're a different race. Veeeeery racist, since it was initially used to mock people of color and play into racist stereotypes—and is sometimes still used that way even today.

RACIST JOKES: Again—if it's making fun of a whole group of people based on the color of their skin, it's bad. End of story.

HATE CRIMES: Crimes (usually ones involving violence) that are motivated by prejudice against a particular group of people.

WHITE SUPREMACY GROUPS: White supremacists believe white people are biologically superior to people of color—and are usually pretty bent on creating racial discord and violently eradicating people of color. And white supremacy groups most definitely still exist today.

MASS INCARCERATION: Aka what some people call the modern-day enslavement of Black people in the US. This typically refers to the historically extreme numbers of Black people (especially Black men) in US prisons, and the disproportionate rates at which Black, Indigenous, and Latinx people are imprisoned compared to white people. Because, ICYMI, even today, very high percentages of Black men (some reports say as many as one in three) end up in jail over the course of their lifetimes. And oftentimes, it's for nonviolent drug offenses that were only ever discovered because a disproportionately high number of police officers patrol majority-Black neighborhoods. (Hint: this is often called overpolicing.)

RACIAL SLURS: Any racial slur is, at its core, used to degrade people of color. Sometimes, they're reclaimed by the people they're used against (such as the n-word), and that's perfectly fine. What's *not* fine is when people who don't belong to that group (such as non-Black people) continue to use racial slurs.

POLICE BRUTALITY: Black men are 2.5 times more likely than white men to be killed by the police during their lifetimes. Police and law enforcement can have racial biases—unfortunately, just like anyone else—but unlike most people, police have the power to inflict extreme damage and brutality based on those biases, which is why police brutality disproportionately impacts Black people.

OPPRESSIVE AND DISCRIMINATORY LAWS: Any laws used to keep a particular group of people down in one way or another. Pretty obviously bad. In the case of BIPOC, a big example is the quality of schools being based on property taxes. Since poverty in the US affects people of color at disproportionate rates, and since property taxes help fund public schools, kids in wealthier, whiter areas get a better education. See the problem here?

STEREOTYPING: Making assumptions about someone due to the color of their skin. It's basically always harmful, because it throws an entire group of people into one box. Even worse: these stereotypes are often used to justify racism, violence, and bigotry.

RACIAL PROFILING: Suspecting someone did something wrong just because of the color of their skin.

CULTURAL APPROPRIATION: This one can get pretty complex. It's when members of a dominant group (usually white people) adopt aspects of another culture not their own, oftentimes for commercial gain or without giving credit or respect where credit and respect are due. It's white privilege at its finest, especially when you consider how people of color are often punished for embracing aspects of their culture—for example, Indian women wearing bindis, or Black people wearing cornrows—because it can be seen as "unprofessional" or maybe even singles them out as being part of that particular culture. But when white people do it, it can be seen as cool.

ASSIMILATION: Feeling pressured into appearing to be part of the dominant group in a society. It can lead to feeling ashamed of your culture and traditions and even casting them aside to fit in.

All of those terms, tropes, and systems we just went through? Each of them falls into the individual/systemic and overt/covert model of looking at racism. Check it out.

OVERT/INDIVIDUAL	COVERT/INDIVIDUAL
Blackface, brownface, yellowface	"You don't sound ____" or "You're so articulate"
Racist jokes	Tokenism
Racial slurs	Racial profiling
White supremacy groups	"I don't see color" or "There's only one human race"
Hate crimes	White savior complex
	Cultural appropriation
	Tone policing

OVERT/SYSTEMIC	COVERT/SYSTEMIC
Mass incarceration	Assimilation
Police brutality	Redlining
Oppressive and	Whitewashing education
discriminatory laws	Racial gerrymandering

Of course, these aren't the only ways that racism plays out—but they are some of the most prominent.

Point being: racism manifests in all kinds of ways, from individual to systemic and from overt to covert. And it can all too easily shift from quietly racist thoughts to violent, majorly horrific acts. See: slavery, police brutality—among many, many others.

Sound similar to what I talked about with xenophobia?

That's not the only similarity between racism and other isms and phobias. One main one is that they can all be systemic. In the case of racism, this means that while people aren't born racist, since racism can be found in pretty much every aspect of society, it lives on. And sadly, it's a whole lot easier for many people to subscribe to racist beliefs than it is to actively fight back against them.

Yep—this ties in to what I talked about in this section's intro.

Fighting back against racism is kind of like fighting back against, well, everything. The why: our society was built on systems intended to keep the people who created them in power. And as long as those systems function as they were meant to function, institutional racism will live on. The good news? We all have the power to help change that.

Nationalism

Nationalism (noun): **identification with one's own nation and support for its interests, especially to the exclusion or detriment of the interests of other nations**

You're not wrong: this sounds very similar to xenophobia. Think of nationalism as one of the causes of xenophobia.

There's a big difference between nationalism and patriotism. Maybe they used to mean sort of a similar thing (see: the French and American Revolutions), but they definitely don't anymore. While patriotism is loving your country, nationalism is waaaaay more extreme and exclusionary. Nationalism is loving your country, and *only* your country—and only the *version* of your country that you think is the ideal. Anyone who doesn't fit that particular ideal (so in US white nationalists' eyes, for example, that would mean anyone who is not white, English-speaking, and Christian) is seen as a threat to the country itself. Which is why nationalism is really a form of hate and, like xenophobia, can all too easily lead to violence.

Yeah. Look out for that throughout this book, too.

Homophobia, Biphobia, and Transphobia

Homophobia (noun): **dislike of or prejudice against homosexual people or queer people in general**

Biphobia (noun): **dislike of or prejudice against bisexual people**

Transphobia (noun): **dislike of or prejudice against transgender people**

LGBTQ+ people are "far more likely than any other minority group in the United States to be victimized by violent hate crime."

That's according to the FBI. It's not just true of the United States—no matter where you go, LGBTQ+ people are one of the most persecuted groups. And it's not just true of history. Homophobia, biphobia, and transphobia are extremely common, right in this moment.

L . . . as in lesbian. Aka women who are attracted to other women. Harmful stereotypes include having short hair, being athletic, and wearing baggy clothes—among others—plus the idea that every lesbian relationship has the "butch" and the "femme." Think: "So, like, which one of you is the guy?"

G . . . as in gay. Aka men who are attracted to other men. Harmful stereotypes include being a pedophile or pervert, having more feminine qualities (including a more female-sounding voice), having a limp wrist, being dramatic, putting traditional and very sexist gender roles onto gay couples (again: "Which of you is the woman?"), and being involved in performing arts. Sometimes, being called "gay"—or being called a f*ggot—is used as an insult.

B . . . as in bisexual. Aka people who are attracted to their own gender and at least one other gender. Harmful stereotypes include being indecisive (especially when it comes to sexual orientation) and being promiscuous.

T . . . as in transgender. Aka people who don't identify with the biological sex assigned to them at birth. Harmful stereotypes include being a pervert, being a drag queen (in the case of trans women), and being more feminine (in the case of trans men). Harmful rhetoric includes not accepting someone's gender and not using their proper pronouns.

Q . . . as in queer or questioning. "Queer" is an umbrella term for many of the terms listed here. It used to be a slur before being reclaimed by LGBTQ+ communities. "Questioning" means you're still figuring things out when it comes to your sexual orientation and/or gender.

+ . . . as in pansexual, asexual, aromantic, omnisexual, intersex, gender-fluid, nonbinary—among others. It leaves the door open to including other sexual orientations and gender identities beyond what I've listed above. There's not a general agreement on what that + entails (some people say it includes straight and cisgender allies, while others don't), but the idea is that it makes things that much more inclusive.

All the harmful stereotypes I just went through? They build and build into a world that has, up until recently, been extremely unfriendly to LGBTQ+ people. And yes—it's not all that friendly now, either. But thanks to the LGBTQ+ rights movement (hint: you'll read a whole lot more about this later in this book), more and more people are fighting homophobia, biphobia, and transphobia than ever before.

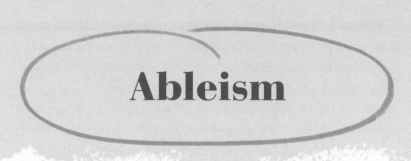

Ableism

Ableism (noun): **discrimination against disabled and neurodivergent people**

If you asked the average person about each of the ten isms and phobias listed in this book, I can bet you that ableism would draw the most blanks. That's kind of an apt comparison to how our world often treats people with disabilities: like they're invisible.

But here's the thing: sixty-one million adults in the United States live with a disability. That's one in four Americans.

It poses an important question. Why do we exist in a society that ignores—and not only that, but actively makes life harder for—a quarter of the population?

To truly understand ableism, you first need to understand what constitutes a disability. Disabilities usually fall into six main categories.

MOBILITY . . . as in serious difficulty walking or climbing stairs.

COGNITION . . . as in serious difficulty concentrating, remembering things, or making decisions.

HEARING . . . as in serious difficulty hearing.

VISION . . . as in serious difficulty seeing.

INDEPENDENT LIVING . . . as in serious difficulty doing errands and other household tasks alone.

SELF-CARE . . . as in serious difficulty doing things like dressing or bathing.

That's according to the Centers for Disease Control and Prevention (CDC), but there is also growing awareness around mental health disabilities, which could include anxiety, depression, attention-deficit/hyperactivity disorder (ADHD), and bipolar disorder . . . to name a few.

Now here are some examples of what constitutes ableism.

MAJOR ABLEISM	"EVERYDAY" ABLEISM
Segregating students with disabilities into different schools and segregating people with disabilities in institutions	Only ever painting disability as tragic or inspirational in the media

Using restraint or seclusion to control people with disabilities	Casting a nondisabled actor to play a person with a disability in a play, movie, commercial, or TV show
Completely disregarding accessibility when it comes to building design plans	Downplaying someone's disability for any reason
Building inaccessible websites, or not providing audio descriptions or closed captioning	Choosing a venue that isn't accessible to people with disabilities
Failing to include braille on signs and elevator buttons . . . among others	Treating someone with a disability like a child (think: talking about them instead of to them, or speaking for them)
Assuming people with disabilities are somehow broken and want or need to be "fixed"	Asking any kind of invasive question about the medical history of someone with a disability
Mocking people with disabilities, using disabilities as a joke, or saying things like "Are you off your meds?"	Automatically assuming someone needs to have a visible disability to be disabled
Using r*tarded in any context	Trying to qualify someone's disability, like "Are you actually disabled?" or "How disabled are you really?" (you get the point)

Straight-up refusing to accommodate people with disabilities, even when they ask	Using the accessible bathroom stall or parking spot if you do not have a disability
Mass murder or abuse of people with disabilities	Calling someone "crazy" or "insane" or "lame" or "stupid" or "dumb"

Unfortunately, many of the above are extremely common, and at times, it can feel like there isn't much effort to make things right.

I'm sure you've heard someone use the r-word, and I'm sure you've entered a building that didn't make it just as easy for someone with a disability to enter. People with disabilities are constantly living lives that are less fair and less just than people who do not have disabilities. It's up to all of us to recognize the inherent ableism in both our actions and our society . . . and then actively work to fight it.

On the road to a more inclusive and equitable society, we all need to remember not to leave people with disabilities behind.

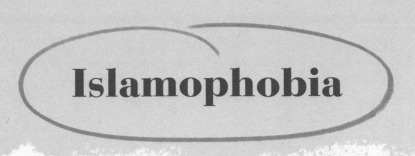

Islamophobia

Islamophobia (noun): **dislike of or prejudice against Islam or Muslims, especially as a political force**

This is the first time in this section that I've brought up an ism or phobia on the basis of religion. You'll see this idea of religious divide and hatred coming up often throughout this book. It's been a big driving force throughout history, and it continues to be a driving force today.

A quick note: a phobia is an exaggerated fear of something. In this case, an exaggerated fear of Muslims. And while Islamophobia has been around for a long time, it probably comes as no surprise that there was a big, big rise in Islamophobia after the 9/11 terror attacks.

You'll hear a lot more about 9/11 later, but for now, I'll make it clear that there was an incredible amount of fear in the world after these attacks. People needed somewhere to direct that fear, which, for many people, became hatred. And because the attacks were carried out by al-Qaeda, an Islamic extremist group, some people took that as an excuse to extend that blame to all Muslims (and others who were perceived as Muslim, even if they actually weren't).

Not fair, of course. But it stuck—and Islamophobia's been even more widespread since.

How, you ask?

First things first: as with racism, there are two kinds of Islamophobia—individual and institutional. Individual Islamophobia is any sort of hateful words or actions directed toward Muslims on a person-to-person level. On the other hand, institutional Islamophobia is when Islamophobia is more subtly embedded in some aspect of society. It may not instantly appear Islamophobic, but trust me—it is. Take a look.

INDIVIDUAL ISLAMOPHOBIA

Stereotyping (thinking a Muslim is a terrorist just because they're, you know, Muslim; automatically thinking Muslims oppress women; and more)

Criticizing Muslim beliefs and being disrespectful of Muslim traditions

Criticizing the wearing of hijabs and other head coverings

Individual acts of violence against Muslims

INSTITUTIONAL ISLAMOPHOBIA

Muslims being portrayed almost always as terrorists in media. (List off as many movies or TV shows as you can that feature a Muslim terrorist. Now list off movies and TV shows that feature Muslims in other roles. Get my point?)

Negative news portrayal (you hear about a lot more instances of Islamic extremist terrorism than, say, terrorism and acts of violence from white people in the US—which are rarely even labeled terrorism in the first place—while positive stories featuring Muslims often get pushed to the side because they don't fit into that whole terrorist narrative)

Laws oppressing Muslims and Muslim traditions (burkini bans at some beaches, immigration laws discriminating against Muslims and majority-Muslim countries . . . you get the idea)

Government acts of violence against Muslims

The thing about institutional Islamophobia is that it's a more widespread, deeply rooted way to oppress Muslims and keep them down. You're right—this also ties in with what I discussed in the beginning of this section about an imbalance of power. Institutional Islamophobia can be born from individual Islamophobia, but it can also keep individual Islamophobia alive by spreading Islamophobic rhetoric to new people.

I'll go into a little more detail about that last one. Take a second to think about how many wars the United States has fought in the Middle East over just the past few decades. Take a second to think about how many civilians (most of whom are Muslim) have been killed by US and US-allied forces in those wars.

That's not an accident. Islamophobia has been used to justify far too many acts of violence in the Middle East, costing tens of thousands of civilian lives. After all, it's a whole lot easier to convince people that a war is worthwhile if those most harmed by the war are generally seen as second-class citizens, as many Muslims in Western societies are.

That unfortunate theme of fear turning into hate, and hate turning into violence, rings true here yet again. And you'll see just how big and global an impact that can go on to have as you read through the chapters ahead.

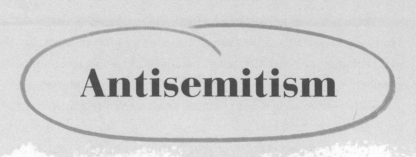

Antisemitism

Antisemitism (noun): **hostility to or prejudice against Jews**

Right off the bat, when you read the word "antisemitism," your mind probably goes to the Holocaust. And yeah. The Holocaust is definitely one of the biggest and most tragic antisemitic acts in history. But it's not the only one—and it unfortunately wasn't the last.

Case in point: in 2018, the FBI released a report on hate crimes. Turns out, nearly 60 percent of religion-based hate crimes in the United States . . . target Jews. Even though Jews only make up about 2 percent of the population. Not only that, but Jewish people have been the most targeted religious group in the US every year since 1991.

That's been a common theme throughout history. For forever, Jews have been one of the world's most persecuted religious groups.

They've been seen as greedy, cheap, deceitful, stingy—the list goes on.

They've been depicted as having horns and big noses.

They've been blamed for pretty much anything you can think of throughout history, from the black death to Germany's economic problems in the early 1900s.

They were violently expelled from countless places over countless centuries. Think: England, France, Spain, Egypt, Iran, what's now Israel . . . basically everywhere.

In medieval times, they were forced to live in Jewish ghettos in many European cities—plus forced to be moneylenders and bankers, since that was considered a dirty job among Christians. Yep, that's where the whole thing about Jews controlling the banks comes from. So there's plenty of antisemitic material throughout history that depicted Jews as less than or secondary to non-Jews.

But, and this is a big *but*, there's also a school of thought, a second type of antisemitism, that says that Jews are, you know, the elite. And that's what makes this version of antisemitism different from every other ism and phobia. It's not based on the idea that Jews are inferior—it's based on the idea that antisemites are actually punching up. Often making it a whole lot harder to identify.

It's like when people say Jews control the media, or Jews are the puppet masters pulling the strings of global power. It twists antisemitism into the kind of thing where antisemites try to argue that they're not being antisemitic—they're just fighting the people on top. But while individual Jewish people have been successful, lumping all Jewish people into that group and saying that gives someone the right to degrade them is antisemitic.

And acts of antisemitism still very much live on, big and small. Here are just a few stats, courtesy of the Anti-Defamation League:

15,694—the number of antisemitic incidents in the US between 2008 and 2019. This includes everything from spray-painting swastikas and defacing Jewish cemeteries to threatening to bomb synagogues and engaging in acts of violence against Jews.

74—the percent of people in Middle Eastern and North African countries who harbor antisemitic views, which is also the case for over a billion people worldwide

41—the percent of people in a worldwide poll across 102 countries who said they believe Jews are more loyal to Israel than to their own country. This is antisemitic because it plays into that concept of "dual loyalty"—that Jews will always be more loyal to Israel or to each other than to their own countries. Which is ultimately very harmful, since it's been used by everyone from modern-day white supremacists (who say it proves that Jews engage in a secret plot to take over the world) to Nazis (who said it proved Jews were traitorous and disloyal) to further antisemitic rhetoric. And while I'm on the subject, it's okay to criticize the Israeli gov, even if you're not Jewish. What's not okay? Using antisemitic stereotypes to criticize Israel's gov, or blaming all Jews for that country's injustices.

A major way in which antisemitism lives on is through white supremacy. Hint: we all know that the Ku Klux Klan violently targeted—and continues to target—Black people, but did you know that they also went after Jews? And modern-day white supremacists, white nationalists, and neo-Nazis continue to spread antisemitic rhetoric and commit acts of violence against Jews. Think: the Pittsburgh Tree of Life synagogue shooting, in which a man screaming antisemitic slurs killed eleven congregants. It was the largest antisemitic attack in US history. And it took place in 2018.

"There is a problem in America with a very strong, powerful

tribal group that dominates our media and dominates our international banking."

That was David Duke, the former leader of the Ku Klux Klan, talking about Jews. Definitely not okay.

But antisemitism is not common just among white supremacist groups. Popular far-left figures like Louis Farrakhan—an American religious leader and political activist—have made a lot of antisemitic comments, too. See: Farrakhan has (falsely) pointed fingers at Jews for apparently controlling the media, being perverts, and having played a big part in the slave trade. Remember that David Duke quote we just read? Here's one just as bad from Louis Farrakhan: "To my Jewish friends, I shouldn't use the word 'friends' so lightly, you have been a great and master deceiver, but God is going to pull the covers all off of you."

The truth is, antisemitism is rampant *wherever* you look. And it's not alone.

You've read about nationalism, and how that can easily shift into a greater fear and hatred toward foreigners. Plus how xenophobia can all too quickly and dangerously escalate to things like war and genocide. You read about how so much of society is built to keep women, people with disabilities, and people of color down. You read about how LGBTQ+ people face all kinds of harmful stereotypes—as do Muslims and majority-Muslim countries.

There's still so much work to be done to dismantle these isms and phobias.

That's where you come in. That's where all of us come in.

Because, like I said, we can't change the world unless we know about it. But once we do? The future is ours for the making.

THE WARS

War is never a straightforward thing.

When you watch movies or TV shows, it sure looks straightforward: People go into battle. They fight. Some people die—but never the hero. The hero kills the villain. The war is over, the world is saved, everyone goes back to their lives.

Only in real life, there's rarely just one villain. In real life, there's rarely just one pinnacle battle. In real life, the heroes die, too. And in real life, things do not just magically go back to normal.

War splits a deep cavern in the earth—a cavern that swallows everyone and everything in sight—and when the people and the countries fighting the war pack up and leave, that cavern remains. Everyday citizens are left to figure out how to climb back out of that cavern and patch it up. And more often than not, they simply can't. The world ignores them and leaves them to suffer, content to forget about the war and move on.

Some people become angry. Hatred brews.

Before you know it, another war is on the horizon.

It's a vicious cycle. You'd think that we would learn, but all you have to do is take one look at the past few decades to know that we haven't.

So it's time we *do* learn. It's time we take it upon ourselves to put an end to this pattern of violence and suffering.

But in order to do that, we need to take a look at what leads to these wars in the first place.

World War II

You know the general story of World War II. Perhaps you know the story of Adolf Hitler and his brutal quest to build an "Aryan race" by invading the rest of Europe and viciously killing six million Jews—not to mention about five million Roma, Jehovah's Witnesses, LGBTQ+ people, Black people, physically and mentally disabled people, political opponents, artists, resistance fighters, and Slavic peoples. Perhaps you know the story of the Allied forces (France, Great Britain, the US, the Soviet Union, and, in part, China), who rose up against Hitler and the Axis powers (Germany, Italy, and Japan). Perhaps you know the story of the ensuing battles, which lasted from 1939 to 1945 and left between forty million and fifty million people dead. Perhaps you know the story of the Normandy landings and D-Day, or the story of Pearl Harbor. Perhaps you know the story of the Japanese American internment camps. And perhaps you know the story of the atomic bombings of Hiroshima and Nagasaki, which ultimately led to the end of history's largest and bloodiest conflict.

Maybe you know all that.

But what you may not know is that some of World War II's greatest impact . . . came as part of its aftermath.

UNITED NATIONS. NATO. COLD WAR. VIETNAM WAR. KOREAN WAR. ISRAEL–PALESTINE CONFLICT.

What do these events all have in common?

They all stemmed, at least in part, from World War II.

Yes, really.

World War II left behind a divided world, but in some ways, it also created a world that was more unified than ever before. See: not even a month after the official end of the war, reps from fifty countries got together in San Francisco to talk peace. And agreed that the whole idea of the Allied forces (multiple countries coming together to fight for a cause) should stick around.

Enter: the United Nations.

The UN was a big deal back then, and it continues to be today. The org serves as a great uniter between most of the world's nations, works toward social progress, prioritizes peace on a global scale, and sets standards for human rights. None of which had really been done before.

But while the United Nations was forming, much of the world was splintering.

Quick refresher: for centuries, European countries had been claiming parts of the world (from India and Pakistan to the Middle East to Africa), colonizing them, and taking not only land, but rights, from those who had already been living there. Think: colonizers like France, Portugal, Great Britain . . . to name a few.

It probably doesn't come as much of a surprise that these colonized countries weren't all that happy with the arrangement. But they couldn't really do much about it, since for the most part, they just couldn't compete with the military prowess of those European countries.

Until World War II.

Which left those European countries so depleted . . . that they pretty much had no choice but to hand over independence.

In the fifteen years that followed World War II, three dozen nations across Asia and Africa claimed independence. Check some of them out on this map.

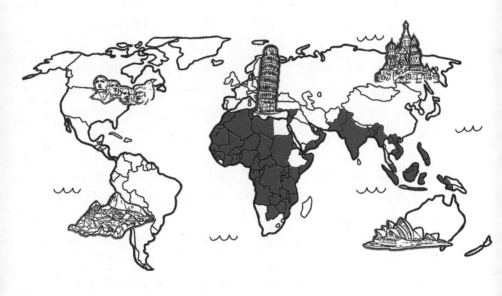

So in that sense, you could say that World War II saw the end of the colonial era, which had dominated the past several hundred years.

But it certainly wasn't the end of revolutions and insurgencies and political conflicts for these newly independent countries—nor was it the end of colonialism as a whole. (Hint: some Portuguese colonies, like Mozambique and East Timor, didn't gain independence until decades later, and there are still some territories around the world held under the control of more powerful countries to this day.)

More on that in a bit.

For now, keep in mind that, for all that World War II was a huge historical event in and of itself, it also had repercussions well beyond the years of, you know, actual battle—repercussions that led to new problems and wars and conflicts, some of which are still ongoing in some form even today.

Liiiike what you're about to read.

The Cold War

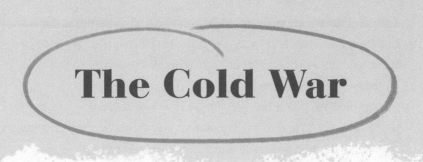

Post–World War II, over in Europe, not all the members of the Allied forces were getting along.

Meet the Soviet Union.

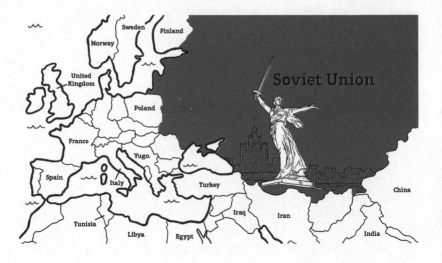

The Soviet Union and the United States disagreed on some things. Read: a lot.

SOVIET UNION	UNITED STATES
SWIPE LEFT: The Soviets were aaaaall for communism, a political and economic theory in which pretty much everything is publicly owned and people are paid based on their abilities and needs.	SWIPE LEFT: The Americans were aaaaall for capitalism, a political and economic system in which bizes are controlled by private owners, rather than by the gov.
SWIPE RIGHT: The Soviets wanted to keep Germany divided to prevent it from rising up again as a threat.	SWIPE RIGHT: The Americans wanted to keep Germany divided to prevent it from rising up again as a threat.
SWIPE LEFT: Buuuut the Soviets thought the best way to do that was by spreading communism.	SWIPE LEFT: The Americans thought the best way to do that was by spreading democracy.
SWIPE LEFT: Even deeper than that, the Soviets didn't like the fact that the US refused to treat the Soviet Union as a legit part of the international community.	SWIPE LEFT: . . . while the Americans didn't like Joseph Stalin, the leader of the Soviet Union, and what they saw as his tyrannical rule of the country.
SWIPE LEFT: Plus the Soviets didn't like that the US entered World War II so late, all while tens of millions of Russians were dying. This was a very, very big point of resentment in the Soviet Union's tumultuous relationship with the US.	SWIPE LEFT: After World War II, the US became increasingly worried that the Soviet Union could try to take over the world and pose a threat to the US's growing global influence. It probably didn't help that the Soviets totally promoted this idea and saw themselves as a revolutionary power.

I'll repeat: there was a long list of reasons the Soviet Union and the United States weren't fans of one another, even during World War II, when they were technically allies. But really, the biggest disagreement came down to the whole communism vs. capitalism thing—and, of course, which system would prevail and give the country backing it more global power.

So once World War II was over, the Soviet Union started installing communist govs throughout Eastern Europe. The US intro'd the Marshall Plan, which let it hand aid to recovering Western European countries (the same deal was offered up to Eastern European countries, but Joseph Stalin shook his head to it). Meaning much of Western Europe was under American influence.

All of this led to . . . the Cold War. (Cue ominous music.)

I should probably start off by saying that the Cold War dominated the second half of the twentieth century. Whatever was happening in the world was almost always in the context of the Cold War. It was unavoidable, it was all-encompassing, and for a lot of the time, it had everyone really freaked out about the possibility of another world war.

Like, really freaked out.

But obviously, this book is called *Cramm This Book*—not *Detail Everything That Ever Happened in the History of Ever This Book*. So I'm going to skimp on some of the deets here in an effort to stick to what's still important all these years later.

Okay. So, it's 1947. World War II just ended a couple years ago. The Cold War's just begun. Tensions between the US and the Soviet Union are already ultra high (because, all those differences I listed out above) and continuing to get higher by the day. And the dynamic between the two countries? Well, it continues to shift drastically—and irreparably. Let's go through the highlights.

First came the Berlin Wall.

It probably doesn't come as much of a surprise that the eyes of the whole world were on Germany following World War II. So the Allied forces got together at two peace conferences (one in Yalta, which was in the Soviet Union, and one in Potsdam, which was in Germany) to chat about the country's future.

Ultimately, they decided to split Germany up into four allied occupation zones, with the Soviet Union taking the eastern part of the country and the US, Great Britain, and (after a little bit of time passed) France taking the western part of the country. Whiiiich also led to Berlin, Germany's capital (located fully inside the Soviet zone), being similarly divided up.

It wasn't just divided along countries; it was also divided along ideologies, with West Berlin being capitalist and East Berlin being communist. This didn't sit well with the Soviet Union, which tried to kick the US, Great Britain, and France—and capitalism—out of Berlin entirely by creating a blockade (which sealed off West Berlin from the outside world). Their goal? Starve West Berlin into defeat.

Now, it's important to keep in mind that the US is really good about not getting involved with something unless there's some sort of ulterior motive, some sort of Other Thing that has the potential to either help or hurt the US in a significant way. If that Other Thing doesn't exist, you can pretty much guarantee the US will plug its ears. A famous example of this is, you know, World War II, when the US kind of let everything slide until Japan attacked Pearl Harbor.

In this case, that Other Thing was communism. If the Soviet Union succeeded at, well, starving West Berlin into defeat, it was all but guaranteed it would adopt the political ideologies of East Berlin. And the US just couldn't let communism move forward anywhere and gain more power.

Cue lightbulb.

The US had an idea, and they were eager to share it with all their allies. So what did that conversation look like?

Let's just imagine for a second that the whole world is high school, with world leaders as high school students. Well, that conversation probably would have gone a little something like this (assuming, of course, that they had cell phones in 1949):

US: omg. it's official: the soviet union is just the worst! did you see what they did in germany with that blockade?

UK: what a bloody wanker! they need to be stopped.

Canada: you know, i don't think we should be gossiping about this, eh? i mean, the soviet union did help us in world war 2 . . .

France: oh, canada, always sooooo nice. don't gossip about this, be kind about that, everyone get along all of the time. enough! vive la france!

US: everyone shut up. i just got the BEST idea.

France: of COURSE you did. vive la france!

Canada: let's hear them out, eh?

US: okay okay okay i am literally so excited about this idea. you're going to love it.

France: the suspense is killing me. vive la france!

UK: get to it!

US: okay, so i'm just spitballing here, but maybe we all form a club?

Canada: an alliance, eh?

US: TOTALLY. that. an alliance. NO. a POLITICAL-MILITARY alliance. and we can invite belgium, denmark, iceland, italy, luxembourg, the netherlands, norway, and portugal to join, too. and we can all make a pact that if we ever have any beef with each other, we can just talk things out. OR if any of us gets attacked, we'll all help out and defend one another. probably against the soviets. because i hate them. did i say that yet?

France: you did. many times. vive la france!

Of course, it didn't go exaaaaactly like that. It obviously didn't happen over text message—and it took a whole lot more effort than one simple conversation. But the result was the same: the formation of the North Atlantic Treaty Organization (aka NATO), an alliance that still stands today and has thirty independent member countries.

Okay. Back to the blockade. In addition to creating NATO, the US, the UK, and France airlifted more and more supplies to West Berlin, rendering the blockade—and the Soviet Union's plan to starve West Berlin—totally useless. About a year after it started, it was called off.

But tensions between the US and the Soviet Union just kept rising. Over in China, communism was also on the rise—and the country was quickly becoming one of the Soviet Union's greatest allies. It was right around this time (1949) that the Soviets . . . exploded their first atomic warhead. Then there was also the Warsaw Pact, which was kind of the Soviet Union's version of NATO and included Albania, Bulgaria, Czechoslovakia, East Germany, Hungary, Poland, and Romania. Oh, and the Space Race was starting up, too. That saw both the US and the Soviet Union, well, racing to conquer the next great frontier: space. It was yet another way in which the two countries weren't exactly buddy-buddy. (And by the way, the Space Race happened in large part because both the US and the Soviet Union thought the other might try to weaponize space, and neither one wanted the other to have the upper hand. Yep—the US and the Soviets first got into space exploration . . . for military reasons.)

So yeah. Long story short: whoever was in charge of covering the Cold War at the newspaper was kept very busy.

Let's get back to Germany.

Ever since that blockade in Germany fell thanks to the Berlin Airlift, refugees from East Berlin started making their way to the West. Nearly three million refugees, to be exact. Something East Germans and the Soviets weren't all that happy about. Add that to the fact that West Germany was admitted as a member of NATO, and the Soviets felt like they needed to do something—and fast.

So on August 13, 1961, the East German gov began construction on a barbed-wire and concrete-block wall along the border between East and West Berlin.

Standoff renewed.

Unlike the blockade, this actually worked. It was pretty impossible to get to the other side of the city unless you passed through a few key checkpoints (about five thousand people did escape between 1961 and 1989, while 171 people died trying).

Okay. Let's put a pin in this for now, because the Berlin Wall clearly wasn't the only thing happening during the Cold War. So here's what else was going on at this time that's definitely super important to know.

Enter: Cuba.

For years, both the US and the Soviet Union had been developing intercontinental ballistic missiles. But it wasn't until 1962 that these missiles truly came into play.

Quick backstory: a year earlier, some people who had been exiled from Cuba and who weren't fans of the country's new leader, Fidel Castro, attempted to invade it. They were financed by none other than the US gov. The invasion—dubbed the Bay of Pigs invasion—failed, but the impact was monumental.

Castro, who had relied on the Soviets for security in the past, asked a favor of the Soviet Union. A favor that involved missiles.

Almost immediately, the US responded by sending military

ships to Cuba and surrounding the island with a blockade. The US prez at the time—John F. Kennedy—said the US was prepped to use force . . . if necessary.

Turns out, the Soviet Union didn't want that. So the two govs struck up a deal. The Soviets agreed to ditch Cuba—so long as the US promised not to invade the island.

You might hear the Cuban Missile Crisis mentioned a whole lot throughout your life, particularly in relation to the political landscape during the 1960s and the ever-present fear of nuclear war, which was arguably at its strongest during that time. You'll also hear about a thing called "mutually assured destruction," which in this case meant that both the US and the Soviets knew that if one of them shot missiles at the other, the other would respond in kind, and they'd both wind up much worse for the wear. This is a big part of what kept the Cold War from becoming an all-out hot war.

Okay. Moving on.

By this point in the Cold War, the Soviet Union and the US each had a pretty extensive list of allies who shared their ideologies. And neither side was willing to give up even a single one of those allies.

Cue a series of (mostly political and nonviolent, but sometimes fully violent) wars being fought around the world. But even as the Soviets fought to keep their allies on Team USSR, they lost arguably the biggest ally of all: China. Here's how that went down:

China: i think we should break up.

Soviet Union: are you kidding me??? i was just going to try to break up with you!

China: i know we've been through a lot, but it's time i focus on myself for once. i have a lot i need to work through.

Soviet Union: that's what i was going to tell you!

Soviet Union: it's not you, it's me.

China: it's not you, it's me.

Soviet Union: stop stealing my lines!

Well. Maybe it went a little bit differently. But the point is: China ditched the Soviet Union . . . and right around the same time, the Soviet Union was cutting ties with China. It was the kind of breakup where both sides just kept on doing things that deeply bothered the other. Think: the Soviets denied financial aid to China, kept its treaty with India even though the country was at war with China, and didn't help China develop a nuclear weapons program.

Okay. Maaaaybe it was mostly the Soviets.

Not only that, but the US's prez in the early '70s, Richard Nixon (a whole lot more on him later), actually took a trip to China—becoming the first US prez to do so.

Just like that, the Soviet Union lost one ally . . . and the US (sort of) gained another—or at the very least, a powerful political tool it could use to pressure the Soviet Union into de-escalating things.

But due to the nature of the Cold War—you know, the fact that neither side could ever truly let things go—while that did lead to some treaties being signed, things didn't stay peaceful for long.

Enter: the 1980s. Both sides started ramping up the building of nuclear arms. And that wasn't all.

Suddenly, a lot was happening all at once. The Soviet Union invaded Afghanistan in an attempt to keep it communist, leading to the death of, well, a lot of people. The estimates range from 562,000 to two million civilians. The US and a bunch of its allies boycotted the Moscow 1980 Summer Olympics in response. The Soviet Union and a bunch of its allies boycotted the Los Angeles 1984 Summer Olympics in response to the response. The US pledged to deploy missiles in West Germany. Then dubbed the Soviet Union an "evil empire." The US and the Soviet Union showed off their military strength by assembling ships and flying aircraft, which basically just served to piss each other off. NATO conducted a very, very realistic simulation of a nuclear attack. Which led the whole world to pretty much freak out.

Tension, high.

Then, just as suddenly . . . everything changed.

Meet Mikhail S. Gorbachev.

Gorbachev, who came into power in 1985, was fundamentally different from all the past leaders of the Soviet Union. He set about dismantling the totalitarian aspects of Soviet society (so all the parts of society that made it more like a dictatorship) and replacing them with a more democratized political system.

Right around Gorbachev's rise to power, more and more Soviet allies (think: Poland, Hungary, and Czechoslovakia) began shifting away from communism and toward democracy. Gorbachev was cool with it. No, really.

And here's why. For decades, the Soviet Union's economy had been sagging dramatically. Really dramatically. People were without homes and food, and instead of investing money in institutions that would help the working class, most resources were being funneled to the military. People were becoming increasingly disillusioned with the idea of communism.

Through the use of propaganda, the gov was usually able to convince people that there was a light at the end of the tunnel. But once they lost all their allies to capitalism and democracy, the situation turned much darker.

Gorbachev didn't fight back, not even a little bit—not even in 1989, when East Berlin declared that its citizens could once again freely cross over to West Berlin, setting off the fall of the Berlin Wall and, one year later, the rise of a unified Germany.

Told you I'd come back to that.

So yes—in a sense, the Cold War started and ended with Germany. But there was still more to come.

Little did the Soviets know, a similar democracy-oriented fate awaited them.

Drumroll, please . . .

Forty-four years after the start of the Cold War, Russia—no longer leading the Soviet Union—now had a democratically elected anticommunist leader (a guy named Boris Yeltsin). I'll repeat: Russia elected a leader who was not a fan of communism. You read that right.

THE END

(I swear.)

Roll end credits:

The Self-Described Hero	The United States
The Supportive Best Friend	NATO
The Villain (as Appointed by the Hero)	The Soviet Union
The Henchman	China
Featuring	Germany, Outer Space, Cuba

Oh, actually . . . one final thing. (I know, I know.)

The Cold War was one of the single most influential conflicts in recent history. It shaped the way our world looks right here, right now.

Well, okay—maybe we don't have a missile crisis or a space race going on at this very instant. But the US's relationship with Russia isn't exactly perfect. The two countries still often find themselves at odds, in terms of both political ideology and global influence.

So whenever you hear people talk about Russia, or the US and Russia, or election interference, or various ongoing conflicts in the Middle East, or literally any number of other things, know that these are Cold War remnants. Its legacy sure isn't cold.

It lives on—in more ways than one.

The Korean War and the Vietnam War

The battle between democracy and communism led to some other wars, too. Two of them were somewhat closely related—and they're both ones that I mentioned earlier, in the World War II chapter. Think: the Korean War and the Vietnam War.

I'll start with Korea. It's 1945. World War II is newly ended. And as was the case with Germany, the Allied forces aren't all that trusting of Japan.

ICYDK, the end of World War II was also the end of the Japanese empire as the world knew it—largely because the Allied forces swept in and occupied the country to oversee a transition to a new political system.

But the Allied forces didn't just occupy Japan. They also occupied the empire's colonies . . . including Korea, which had been under Japanese control since 1905.

Here's another similarity to Germany in the aftermath of World War II. The US took one-half of Korea, and the Soviet Union took the other.

Koreans didn't exactly expect to be occupied and divided. In fact, it was a traumatic shock to the country, which had been united for

Russia

Mongolia

North
Korea

China

Vietnam

South
Korea

Taiwan

Japan

Philippines

more than a thousand years. They thought they'd be liberated and left to govern themselves—like other victims of the Axis powers, such as France.

You can probably see where this is going.

The Soviet Union pretty much instantly made their side—the north—communist. Because, you know, their whole thing about thinking communism was the solution to all the world's problems, and also their whole thing about wanting to have more global power over the US. Meanwhile, the south was home to a US-supported military gov.

The general plan was to ditch Korea once everything was smoothed over with Japan.

But here's the thing: the US and the Soviet Union, in case you couldn't tell, really did not trust each other. At all. Both sides were worried about which side Korea would be on once all the internal politics were sorted out. Either way, at the very beginning of the occupation of Korea, there was still talk about ways to compromise on how to govern it.

But then the Cold War barged in and basically ruined all that.

If the relationship between the US and the Soviet Union had been chilly before, the Cold War plunged it deep into the Arctic. Talks went into deadlock. Neither wanted to risk giving up Korea to the enemy.

Remember the United Nations? They start to come into play here.

United States: omg. the soviets are being literally impossible.

United Nations: *sighs* what is it now, america?

US: they're like totally ghosting me!

UN: and . . . ?

US: maybe you could talk to them for me?

UN: . . .

US: please please please PLEASE PLEASE PLEASE PLEASE.

UN: okay, okay! just what do you want me to say.

US: okay, so you know how the soviets are in korea, and i'm in korea? at first it was like, oh, we're totally going to be out of here soon. but then we got in a fight, blah blah blah . . . and now i'm not going to leave, and they're not going to leave, and i WANT to leave, but i don't want them to KNOW that i wanna leave.

UN: so . . . ?

US: will you sponsor a vote? so the koreans can decide for themselves what they want, and i can finally get out of there?

UN: sure. why not. if it gets you to stop bugging me about this.

US: omg thank you!!!!! you're seriously the best. :)

UN: don't thank me yet. first, we need to see if the soviets are in.

Spoiler alert: they weren't. That put the UN in a dilemma. Either leave the situation as is . . . or oversee a vote in only the south. The UN chose the vote, and a separate South Korean gov was born.

This did not go over well with the north, which quickly formed *its* own gov, which was largely communist and still totally backed by the Soviet Union.

Intro the Korean War.

I'll cut to the chase: in 1950, about seventy-five thousand soldiers from the North Korean People's Army invaded South Korea in a bid to undo the division by force. (And, hint: this was the first real military action of the Cold War. See how everything's all interconnected?) About a month later, the US was back in South Korea to try to help fend off the north.

But for the US, it was pretty much still all about communism. The country saw this battle as one of the first in what would turn out to be a very, very long war against the political ideology itself, and against the influence that it gave to the Soviets.

The fighting between the north and the south went back and forth, and despite nearly five million fatalities, the front lines ended up pretty much where they started. Over on the US's end, the country was getting increasingly worried that the battle could lead to World War III, just a few years after the end of World War II. So they talked peace with North Korea—and in 1953, the guns fell silent.

But the Korean War never officially ended.

What happened in 1953 was just an armistice agreement (aka a truce) . . . all sides were supposed to sign off on a peace agreement a few months later. But nobody could agree on how to glue Korea back together.

Fast-forward to today, and the Korean peninsula remains divided. The two Koreas and the US all agree there should ultimately be peace. But they still don't agree on the way to get there—and tensions remain high.

But before I get into the world's current political climate (don't worry, that's just a chapter or two away), there's another big war that took place right around this time. And—surprise, surprise—this one has to do with communism vs. democracy, too.

Yes, you guessed it: the Vietnam War. You may have heard a bit about this war over the course of your life, but like basically everything else I've mentioned so far, its roots go all the way back to World War II.

So, it's 1940. The Second World War is hardly a year old. Suddenly, Japan decides to invade Vietnam, which has been under French colonial rule since the 1800s.

Let's dive in to see what happened next.

Say hello to Ho Chi Minh. He was a Vietnamese political leader who took a lot of inspiration from Chinese and Soviet communism. (Yep—there's that magic word again.) He was also, above all, a big fan of the idea of Vietnam getting its independence, so even more than being a communist, he was a nationalist.

That's why he formed the Viet Minh (aka the League for the Independence of Vietnam), bided his time, and . . . took control of the northern city of Hanoi as soon as Japan ditched Vietnam at the end of World War II. He wasn't the only one with his eye on Vietnam. See: France was eager to take back control of the country.

With Japan now out of the picture, Vietnam's official leader was Emperor Bao Dai. And, key thing to know about this guy: he had a French education. Making him a much more appealing option to France than Ho Chi Minh. It wasn't long before the French gov sided with the emperor and established the city of Saigon as the capital of the new state of Vietnam (1949). Another important thing to note: Bao Dai was a total puppet of the French, with virtually no real power or independence.

So here we were again, with half the country communist and half the country buddied up with the West.

You can probably figure out what happened next.

Fighting. A lot of it.

Things went back and forth for a while before Ho and Bao Dai signed off on a treaty that split Vietnam between north and south.

Everything was looking up ... until this guy named Ngo Dinh Diem, who was very much not a fan of communism, waltzed in, took Bao Dai's place, and became prez of what was known at the time as South Vietnam.

It was right around this time, in 1954, when the US decided to get involved on an even greater scale than just providing support to France, which it had already been doing.

Quick refresher: the US's relationship with the Soviet Union was getting rockier and rockier during this time period. And it was getting increasingly worried about the effect communism could have on the world. Specifically, the US was concerned about this thing called the "domino theory," which was the idea that if one Southeast Asian country turned communist, aaaaaall the others would follow.

Cue the US pressing the panic button.

Over the coming years, the US pledged its support to Diem and upped its military presence in Vietnam in what escalated into the Vietnam War. A big turning point? The assassination of Diem in 1963—and the North Vietnamese attacks on two US destroyers in the Gulf of Tonkin in 1964, which prompted the US to retaliate by bombing military targets in North Vietnam.

What followed were more bombings. And more bombings. And more bombings. Not just in North Vietnam, but also in neighboring Laos in an attempt to disrupt Ho's flow of supplies. It left Laos the most heavily bombed country per capita ... in the world.

But it didn't end at bombing. In 1965, the US sent combat forces into battle in Vietnam.

There are many, many layers to what went on in Vietnam. Two million Vietnamese civilians died—with more than four hundred unarmed civilians being slaughtered by US soldiers in the My Lai Massacre alone. Twelve million were forced to become refugees. Hundreds of thousands of US soldiers deserted, and 58,220 were killed. And all this time, as both US public dissent and international dissent grew (more on that later), the fighting, the bombings, the war went on.

Which brings us to January 1973. Richard Nixon was the US's prez, and he clearly noticed that Americans were increasingly opposed to the Vietnam War. Like basically all leaders, he really wanted to keep his hold on power—so Nixon put two and two together and . . . shook hands on a final peace agreement with North Vietnam, after which he slowly but surely withdrew US troops from the country.

While this wasn't the end of fighting between North and South Vietnam (that didn't take place until two years later, when the north seized Saigon, which they renamed Ho Chi Minh City, and claimed victory), it was the end of the US's involvement.

Quick rewind.

Because even though the Vietnam War is over, it still remains one of the most contentious wars in American history. It sparked a whole new conversation about the US's tendency to get involved in arguably unnecessary and prolonged wars. (Hint: you'll hear more about this coming up, when I talk about wars in Afghanistan and Iraq.)

But that's only one legacy of this war.

Another? It fundamentally shifted the US's relationship with China.

ICYMI—the US wasn't the only foreign country to play a major role in the Vietnam War. China—which at the time was still cool with the Soviet Union—did, too.

I'll remind you: China was communist. And, like the Soviet Union, China wanted to see communism spread basically everywhere. So it was all too willing to help out North Vietnam (and had done the same with North Korea earlier on, too).

But a couple decades later? Nixon, you'll remember, was literally in China and working toward a friendlier relationship.

You only need to look at the state of the US's relationship with China in the late 2010s to the early 2020s to know that friendly(ish) relationship didn't exactly last. But the point is: the mid to late 1970s were just the start of a US-China relationship marked by lots of ups and downs. The dynamic between two of the world's most powerful countries was established and linked in more ways than one—and their fates continue to be connected today.

Whether they like it or not.

The Israel-Palestine Conflict

Okay. So I gave you the deets on the Cold War, the Vietnam War, and the Korean War. But there's yet another big conflict that happened at least in part as a result of World War II—and it's still impacting the world today. Majorly.

With Gaza violence "escalating as we speak," UN envoy calls for "immediate stop" (United Nations)

Opinion: Any Solution to the Israeli-Palestinian Conflict Will Lead to Civil War (Haaretz)

Israel and Gaza May Be on the Verge of War. It Could Be Worse than in the Past. (Vox)

Q: So, how did we get here? How did things spiral into what they are today?
A: Well, first off—all the wars you've read about thus far have been pretty crammed, but this time around, let's do a bit of a deeper dive to really get a full grasp on this conflict (but even then, there's not enough space in the world to cover every deet here). Everyone has an opinion on it. Everyone has a different narrative and a different

set of facts and figures. The entire conflict is just riddled with debate. Perhaps you're pro-Israel or pro-Palestine (or both), or perhaps you haven't quite figured that out yet. But regardless, there's usually much more to a story than meets the eye.

This conflict even starts with a debate—namely, over when the Israel-Palestine conflict actually started. That's because the roots of the conflict go back centuries.

Quick refresher: Israel is considered the ancestral homeland of the Jewish people. Enter: the Jewish diaspora. Aka Jews were kicked out of Jerusalem (one of Israel's major cities) and, more generally, Israel. Multiple times. Over the course of millennia.

That left the Jewish people scattered throughout various corners of the world, with many ultimately residing in Europe (but some also in the Middle East, Africa, and Asia). They didn't have it much easier in most of those places (remember the Antisemitism chapter?).

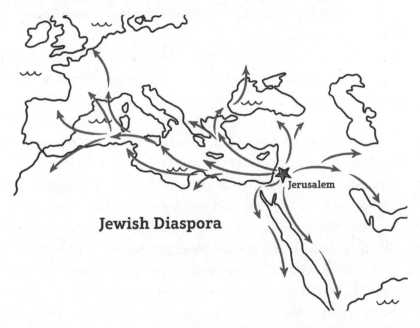

Jewish Diaspora

Here's where Israel-Palestine starts to come into play again. ICYMI, the Ottomans ruled over the land (then called Palestine) from

1516 to 1917. There was a pretty small Jewish population there, but over the course of those four hundred years, that population grew larger and larger as more Jews immigrated to the land.

They built the first modern Jewish neighborhood outside the walled city of Jerusalem (and, in the 1880s, also started establishing small communities across Palestine).

Meanwhile, Jerusalem itself shifted to a Jewish majority.

The Hebrew language was revived in daily use.

It was right around the late 1800s and early 1900s when antisemitism—already very, very high in Europe—started coming to a head. All of a sudden, a Jewish homeland seemed like a pretty great alternative to Europe for the 90 percent of Jews who lived there. And yes: this all took place even before World War II and the Holocaust. Figures like Theodor Herzl, who founded modern political Zionism (aka the movement to re-establish, develop, and protect Israel as a Jewish national homeland), were encouraging Jews to immigrate to Palestine in the late 1800s.

So fast-forward to 1917. World War I was nearing its end. So was the Ottoman rule of Palestine (and also other large swaths of land in that area).

But first: in an effort to get Jews on the side of the Allied powers during the First World War, Britain issued the Balfour Declaration. This basically said that the British supported the idea of "the establishment in Palestine of a national home for the Jewish people." It alsoooo said that "nothing shall be done which may prejudice the civil and religious rights of existing non-Jewish communities in Palestine." Point being: they believed Jews should get an official homeland—but not at the expense of other groups already living there. And for the most part, everyone was cool with this plan . . . especially since the Brits were going around making the same promise to the Muslim leaders of the surrounding Arab countries (see: the Hussein-McMahon correspondence). You read that right—Britain was essentially offering the land to both sides at the same time.

1918. World War I ends. Britain seizes control of Palestine. Intense riots break out between Jews and Arabs living there. There is a huge power struggle for control of the land.

Just twenty-one years later, World War II starts.

I'll repeat: at this point, lots of Jews had immigrated to Palestine (hence those riots I just mentioned). But once World War II hit, even more fled to the land.

The local Arab population was not a fan of this increased migration. They saw it as a European colonial movement. Cue even more vicious fighting that seemed to be beyond anyone's control.

Pay attention. Because in an attempt to fix things, this—right here—this is where the conflict really got out of control.

1947

The United Nations Special Commission on Palestine weighs in. It recs the partition (or divide) of Palestine into a Jewish and an Arab state. The idea is to curb the violence while still letting both groups have a claim to the land, with Jews taking about 53 to 56 percent of the land and Arabs getting the rest. As far as Jerusalem is concerned, it's decided that the city—which is important not just to Judaism, but also to Islam and Christianity—will get international control.

The timing is right. World War II ended a few years ago, and much of the Western world agrees that the Jewish people deserve a country of their own where they will be safe.

Meanwhile, Great Britain's mandate (aka rule) over Palestine is set to end in 1948—opening the door to secure a state for both Jews and Arabs.

The Partition Resolution—or, officially, Resolution 181—passes. Israeli Jews pull out the streamers. Arabs . . . do not.

1948

The British mandate is officially over. Israel declares independence and RSVPs yes on its invite to the United Nations.

Only a slight problem . . . while Israeli Jews nodded their heads to the Partition Resolution, Arabs never did. So almost as soon as Britain packs its bags and leaves, a war breaks out.

A lot happens all at once. Neighboring countries get involved. Egypt, Jordan, Syria, Lebanon, and Saudi Arabia invade Israel.

The Israelis fight back. The war between all the countries is brutal. See: 750,000 Palestinian Arabs escape the area . . . or are expelled, in many cases forcibly. They don't go far. Many head to Lebanon or Jordan with the intention of returning home sometime soon—but most never get the chance.

1949

The war ends with a ceasefire. In the process, Israel gets even more territory than it previously had. Think: nearly 80 percent of the original British mandate. Not a typo. Meanwhile, Jordan takes control

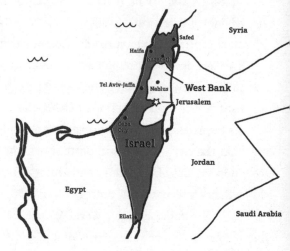

of the West Bank and eastern Jerusalem, while Egypt occupies Gaza. Most of the Palestinians who remained within the borders of the original British mandate settle in one of those two territories. Some, however, stay put in the new country of Israel and become citizens.

It's important to note that Israelis see this as their war of independence . . . while Palestinians today refer to it as the Nakba.

Or the Catastrophe.

Over the next couple decades, up to a million Jewish refugees and immigrants—mostly from Muslim-majority countries (many of which actually kicked out Jewish people when Israel was formed), not to mention around 250,000 Holocaust survivors—make their way to Israel. The country's gov is initially swayed to the (center) left.

All the while, the fighting goes on, including another battle based around a conflict over Egypt's Suez Canal in 1956. The why: there was never any sort of peace agreement after the 1948–1949 war—and the surrounding countries still aren't fans of Israel's presence, or its creation in the first place.

1964

The Palestine Liberation Organization (aka the PLO) is born, with the goal being the "liberation of Palestine." The means: armed struggle designed to fight back against displacement and Israeli military actions. Much of the violence initially targets Israeli citizens.

1967

Let's go back to the Suez Canal. For about ten years, Israel, France, and Britain have been hanging out there. Because, trade. The United Nations also got involved and set up a buffer force in the Sinai Peninsula and Gaza to keep things (somewhat) civil.

So fast-forward to 1967, and Egypt kicks the United Nations buffer force out of the Sinai. Then closes the Straits of Tiran to Israeli shipping.

Israel is outraged.

A violent war breaks out between Israel, Egypt, Jordan, and Syria. It lasts six days, but the effect is astronomical. Just like the 1948–1949 war between Israel and neighboring Arab countries, this one leaves

Israel forcibly taking a lot more land. As in the West Bank, Gaza, the Golan Heights, and the Sinai. Not to mention all of Jerusalem, versus just half—including the part with some of the holiest sites in the world to multiple religions.

Big deal, for many, many reasons—one of which includes the formation of Israeli Jewish settlements in these areas. Yep, that's still a source of tension today.

1972

The Munich Olympics.

Palestinian gunmen take the Israeli team hostage.

Murder two members.

German authorities attempt a rescue.

The gunmen kill nine more Israeli members.

1973

Egypt and Syria join together to launch an attack against Israeli forces in the Sinai and the Golan Heights in what's dubbed the Yom Kippur War or October War. Yet again . . . they lose. But Israel's losses are devastating. Suddenly, for literally the first time ever, support for the dominant, center-left party (the Labor Party) slips.

1977

I'll remind you: Israel is led by a center-left party. Scratch that, because in 1977, a right-wing party (the Likud) wins the country's election. Everyone is shocked. This increasingly comes into play as time goes on and the Likud, which openly gives the thumbs-up to settlements, gains even more power.

About six months after the election, another big political moment takes place. Egypt's prez takes a trip to Jerusalem and talks diplomacy. Israel nods its head to ditching Sinai—plus pledges to expand Palestinian self-gov in the West Bank and Gaza.

The same year, Israel and Egypt sign off on the US-brokered Camp David Accords, which lay the groundwork for a historic peace treaty between the nations a couple years later.

1982

A Palestinian militant group tries to assassinate the Israeli ambassador to London. In response, Israel invades Lebanon to kick out PLO leadership. The invasion is violent. The results are unimaginably grave, with hundreds of Israelis and thousands of Palestinians killed.

Israel sticks around in the country until 1985—but, even after that, keeps occupying a slim "security zone" along the border.

1982's violence doesn't let up. A militia sympathetic to the Kataeb Party (aka the Lebanese Phalanges Party, which is a Christian political party in Lebanon) massacre Palestinians in refugee camps in the capital, Beirut. And the massacre is tied to Israel's defense minister, Ariel Sharon. He is nicknamed the "Butcher of Beirut."

Huge protests break out in Israel.

1987

The situation keeps intensifying. The First Intifada, a Palestinian uprising the likes of which has never been seen before, is born. Chaos breaks out.

The uprising starts out peaceful, with Palestinians taking part in mass boycotts and shaking their heads to working in Israel. But it soon turns into attacks on Israelis, with Palestinians using rocks, Molotov cocktails, and even firearms.

The Israeli military—which has access to more sophisticated weapons—responds in turn.

The death toll weighs heavy on both sides, but significantly more so for Palestinians.

This uprising also sees the rise of Hamas—which is formed by the Muslim Brotherhood, a Sunni Islamist religious, political, and social movement—in Gaza. ICYDK, Hamas is a Palestinian Islamist political organization and militant group that's hugely against Israel. Think: the group calls for the total destruction of the country. You read that right.

The formation of Hamas is a very, very big deal.

You'll want to remember this.

1993

Israel's Labor Party prime minister, Yitzhak Rabin, and the leader of the PLO, Yasser Arafat, shake hands on the Oslo Accords. Which basically make a pact to end the Intifada and work toward a self-governing Palestinian society. You're right—that means Israel nods its head to a phased withdrawal from much of the West Bank and Gaza.

Problem, since some extremist Palestinian and Jewish groups don't like the Oslo Accords. They don't want any sort of compromise, at least not if it means they won't get all of the land controlled by Israel.

Violence continues.

1994

It happens. (Sort of.)

Israel withdraws from most of Gaza and the West Bank city of Jericho.

The PLO moves its base and sets up the Palestinian Authority, which is a self-governing body.

And not long after, Jordan and Israel sign off on a peace treaty.

1995

More signatures are made. See: Israel signs the Interim Agreement, which shifts more power and territory to the Palestinian Authority. This sets off a chain reaction of even more treaties, agreements, and policies, all of which are working toward peace.

Don't get too comfortable.

It doesn't last long.

Because in November of 1995, Yitzhak Rabin, the prime minister of Israel . . . is assassinated.

The murder takes place at the end of a rally in Tel Aviv celebrating the Oslo Accords. And the murderer is a Jewish Israeli ultranationalist who is very much against the idea of any sort of peace and especially hates the Oslo Accords.

The assassination pays off—at least for the murderer. Because the next year . . .

1996

. . . the Likud makes a comeback. And there's a pretty big chance you'll recognize its leader's name.

Cough, **Benjamin Netanyahu**, cough.

All of a sudden, everything changes. Netanyahu (aka Bibi) pledges to cut back on further concessions to and negotiations with Palestinians. Then starts up settlement expansion again.

This is the beginning of a very big, very deadly, and potentially irreversible escalation in the Israel-Palestine conflict.

This escalation is not necessarily immediate. But the Likud's new prominence in gov kinda sorta sets it in motion.

2000

This year sees a lot of sudden change.

Israel ditches southern Lebanon. That's a de-escalation . . .

. . . but just a few months later, things take a few steps back. Israel and the Palestinian Authority have trouble agreeing on things like the timing and the extent of potential further Israeli withdrawal from the West Bank. Talks break down.

It keeps getting worse and worse.

Remember Ariel Sharon? The Israeli defense minister who was tied to the 1982 massacre? Now he's the leader of the Likud. In 2000, he heads to what's known to Jews as the Temple Mount and what's known to Muslims as al-Haram al-Sharif. A very, very holy place for both religions, BTW. Which also makes it a very, very contentious place.

Add in a guy like Sharon to a place like that, and you've got a tense situation.

To say the least.

The opposition leader shows up at the Temple Mount/al-Haram al-Sharif surrounded by hundreds of riot police. And he is greeted by crowds of furious Palestinians who yell "Murderer!" and throw chairs, stones, trash cans, and more at the Israeli forces . . . who retaliate with tear gas and rubber bullets. One protester is shot in the face.

The protests don't stop there. In fact, a new period of violence—what's known as the Second Intifada—is pretty directly linked to this visit.

2002

. . . the intensification of a wave of Palestinian suicide bombings. These had already been happening around Israel, but they become increasingly common over the coming years. And they create an atmosphere for Israelis that is filled with constant fear.

Fear of going on buses.

Fear of sitting in cafés.

Fear of dancing in nightclubs.

Fear of even just walking down the streets of their cities and neighborhoods.

Because you never know where the next bombing might take place.

The Israeli army responds in turn by launching Operation Defensive Shield in the West Bank. It's the largest military operation there since 1967. Not a typo.

But Israel doesn't leave it at Operation Defensive Shield. The threat of more suicide bombings—and attacks from extremist Palestinians in general—feels imminent.

So Israel builds a barrier.

Around the West Bank, to be exact.

And for all that the barrier does help decrease violence, it also raises a loooot a lot of problems—in particular, the barrier doesn't exactly stick to the pre-1967 ceasefire line, also known as the Green

Line, so Palestinians feel like Israel's trying to grab more land (which they have done before). Plus there's the issue of passage between the West Bank and Israel (and, more broadly, passage between Palestinian land and Israeli land), which is heavily regulated and makes a lot of Palestinians feel like second-class citizens.

Because, you know, they effectively are. With this new barrier up, they can't travel to things like jobs, schools, and hospitals—all of which used to be easily accessible. And in general, they have fewer legal and civil rights than Israelis living in the West Bank. Even their roads and checkpoints take longer to get through than the Israeli ones. Many Palestinians even refer to this barrier as an "apartheid wall."

Life for every Palestinian in the West Bank becomes exponentially harder.

If you've heard anything about the Israel-Palestine conflict as it is today, chances are you've heard about just how controversial this barrier continues to be.

One other thing that happened in 2002? The Saudis proposed the Arab Peace Initiative, which was a proposal to end the conflict not just with the Palestinians but with the Arab world at large. Many Arab states endorsed it, but Israel refused to even consider it.

2003

The United States, the European Union, Russia, and the United Nations—aka the Quartet—step in and come up with a road map to put an end to the Israel-Palestine conflict once and for all. (Spoiler alert: it doesn't work.) Their plan? Form an independent Palestinian state.

Everyone is on board. No, really. Both Israel and the Palestinian Authority nod their heads to the plan, which also mandates that Palestinians need to stop attacking Israelis and that Israel needs to halt expansion of West Bank Jewish settlements.

2004

The International Court of Justice gives Israel a little heads-up that the West Bank barrier isn't exactly all that legal.

2005

There's an excruciatingly fleeting moment of de-escalation. (Notice a pattern?)

Israel pulls aaaaaall Jewish settlers and military personnel from Gaza. But keeps control over airspace, coastal waters, and border crossings.

That raises some problems. Hint: Israel kinda sorta does this . . . without coordinating with the Palestinian Authority. In fact, the group is so caught off guard that it gives Hamas the chance to take power.

2006

As in Hamas suddenly moves from being a kind of fringe political group . . . to literally being the Gaza-based Palestinian gov.

I'll repeat: Hamas wins the Palestinian parliamentary elections in Gaza.

Yes, really.

Gaza pretty quickly fires rockets at Israel. (Remember, Hamas isn't for a solution in which both Israelis and Palestinians get their own countries. They want the total destruction of Israel.)

It's also important to remember that a big portion of Palestinians—like, every Palestinian in the West Bank—are still led by the Palestinian Authority, which is for peace (and continues to be today).

The same year, a group of Hamas gunmen take an Israeli soldier—Gilad Shalit—hostage and demand the release of Palestinian prisoners. Cue major, major, major clashes between Israel and Hamas in Gaza.

As I move on to 2007, it's super important to note that lots of Israelis were opposed to the whole Israel-withdraws-from-Gaza thing in the first place. When Hamas slid right in and took over—basically as a direct result of the withdrawal—it gave those Israelis an argument against withdrawal from the West Bank. An argument that's still used today.

2007

The whole idea of a two-state solution—while it existed in theory before—is more clearly established at what is called the Annapolis Conference. And much of the world now sees this as the basis for future talks between Israel and the Palestinian Authority.

2008

Israel launches a full-scale invasion of Gaza.

It lasts nearly a month.

The goal? Keep Hamas and other groups from attacking Israel with rockets, which they have been doing incessantly and without any care of who or what they hit—military targets or schools and homes, soldiers or children . . . it was pretty much all fair game as far as Hamas was concerned.

And just like that, so much of what Israel and the Palestinian Authority had been working toward for the past couple decades is erased. That's particularly devastating, since Israel's prime minister and the Palestinian Authority's leader were thiiiiiis close to reaching a comprehensive peace agreement.

Not only that, but the invasion also served to create what was essentially a large-scale outdoor prison for nearly two million

Palestinians. From this point on, Israel controls every human and vehicle moving in and out of the territory.

There is no hope. No economy. No drinkable water. There is hardly any space—Gaza is a tiny strip of land, and it's one of the most densely populated areas on Earth. The Israel-Palestine conflict has always been closely tied to human rights, but now more than ever before, that's put on display for the whole world to see.

2009

The Likud has a very, very good election day. Netanyahu is back, and he puts together a majority right-wing gov.

2011

Hamas releases Israeli soldier Gilad Shalit, who's been kept hostage since 2006 (so that's five years), in exchange for 1,027 Palestinian prisoners. Germany and Egypt set up the deal.

2012

More and more rocket attacks (launched by groups based in Gaza) target Israeli towns. Read: thousands. Literally. Six people are killed. Israel strikes back with a weeklong military campaign. Many more Palestinians are killed.

The deaths are tragic, regardless of which side you're looking at. And this is what's at the heart of the Israel-Palestine conflict and why it's so incredibly controversial—not just among Israelis and Palestinians, but around the world.

Some people hear this story and see the rocket attacks on Israeli towns and innocent Israeli citizens. Some people hear about this story and see the disproportionate Israeli military response, which leaves innocent Palestinians dead. There are arguments here of liberation and self-defense, aggressor and victim. Everyone has a different opinion on which side is which.

That right there is where those few extremists start to make things even more dangerous. Because to people and groups like Netanyahu and the Likud (and those even further to their right, who have steadily been gaining power), these attacks fit a narrative of senseless and unprovoked violence coming from Gaza. And to people and groups like Hamas, these attacks fit a narrative of a brutal Israeli military regime attacking innocent Palestinian civilians. And underpinning it all, as with all of these wars, is a question of who has power and control over the land and the people who live there.

I want to be clear: I'm definitely not trying to make any direct comparisons here or create a false equivalence. But this is yet another instance when the narratives diverge while discussing the same events and issues, and to understand where we are right now with this conflict, it's very, very important to recognize how the various parties involved see it playing out.

Watch out for this throughout the rest of this conflict, as attacks escalate and international opinion grows.

2014

Armed groups in Gaza launch attacks (again). Israel responds with a military campaign that knocks out missile launching sites (which often happen to be based among civilian populations, meaning more civilians are killed) and tunnels leading from Gaza to Israel (aka attack tunnels). Lots of clashes follow. The violence ultimately ends with a ceasefire brokered by Egypt.

2015

An Israeli couple are shot dead in their car in the part of the West Bank that's under Israeli military occupation. The shooting ushers in a new wave of shootings, stabbings, and car-rammings targeting Israelis and carried out by Palestinians and Israeli Arabs.

2016

The United States renews military aid to Israel in a $38 billion deal. Yes, you read that right: renews. Over the years, the US has been a powerful ally for Israel—and vice versa.

That relationship is put to the test just months later, when the United Nations Security Council passes a resolution condemning settlement building. Israel cuts working ties with a dozen of the countries involved in the vote.

The Security Council has tried passing this kind of a resolution in the past—to which the US always said "veto." But this time around, the US basically just quits the vote instead, making it the first and only time that then-Prez Obama doesn't veto. Plot twist.

2017

Israel's parliament passes a law formally legalizing dozens of Jewish settlements built on private Palestinian land in the West Bank.

Not long later, construction gets started on the first new Jewish settlement there in twenty-five years. (But like everything in this conflict, it's not exactly that straightforward. Rogue settlers have been constructing homes illegally in this area for years. Plus existing settlements have been expanding their borders and taking control of more and more land. To be extra exact, this new settlement is really just the first new *sanctioned* one.)

You can probably imagine that this news is not very well received by Palestinians.

The same month, Israelis get some news that doesn't exactly make them very happy, either. See: UNESCO votes to declare the Old City of Hebron a Palestinian World Heritage site—something Israel says completely erases the city's Jewish heritage.

For the record, this is yet another really good example of why the Israel-Palestine conflict is so fraught. It centers on a swath of land that is home to lots of places, like Hebron, and Jerusalem, and tons of others, that are very, very sacred and holy to several different religions. There are so many different motivations at play here. So much to lose, so much to gain, and a conflict that goes back decades and perhaps even centuries.

Even more happens this year. At this point, Donald Trump is the US's prez—and he and Netanyahu kind of have a bromance. So this year, Prez Trump officially recognizes Jerusalem—not Tel Aviv—as the capital of Israel. That's something Netanyahu's been working toward for a while, always with a lot of pushback from people who say half of Jerusalem technically belongs to Palestinians under the original 1947 United Nations Partition Plan.

2018

Then Prez Trump takes things a step even further . . . and recognizes Israeli sovereignty over the Golan Heights. Reminder: Israel took control of the Golan Heights from Syria in the 1967 war and later annexed the area.

The international community as a whole totally disagrees with Prez Trump and Israel on this, BTW.

That same year, there's another upsurge in violence on the Gaza border.

By now, thousands upon thousands of people have died in the Israel-Palestine conflict—the vast majority of whom are Palestinians killed in Israeli attacks. See: about 25,000 Israelis and more than 90,000 Palestinians.

2019

Netanyahu—who is still at this point Israel's prime minister and the leader of the Likud—is charged with bribery, fraud, and breach of trust in cases unrelated to the Israel-Palestine conflict. But this is still something to keep in mind, because, ICYDK, a fair number of Israelis really don't like Netanyahu. That point is proved even more as the country goes through multiple elections and keeps ending up with a tie between Netanyahu and his various center and center-left opponents . . . until 2021, when Netanyahu is ousted from office and a new gov, with a mix of leaders from across the political spectrum, comes into power. Jury's still out on how much progress they'll be able—or even willing—to make on this conflict.

So there you have it. The general overview of the Israel-Palestine conflict, from start to . . . well, not finish, but where we are now (or, at least, as of this writing).

There's so much more that can't even be contained within this timeline, because it's not just a singular event. But ICYMI, there are two common threads running through each of these years. One of them is Jewish/Israeli self-determination and security. The other is the abuse of the Palestinian people.

It's easy to argue that the Jewish people have a right to a homeland of their own, to live in safety and peace, and that this right has been made very difficult by overtly hostile regional neighbors who have shown time and again that they have no interest in allowing this piece of land to belong to a group of people beleaguered by centuries of persecution and trauma.

But it's also important to consider the cost—and it's steep. Because, at its simplest, while these battles are being waged over pieces of land, so many of the consequences are suffered by Palestinian citizens who have seen their rights eroded over the course of decades and who just want to go about living their lives.

It's hard to convey just what life is like for Palestinians living in Gaza and the West Bank. Really, they're not much more than prisoners.

They can't move as they please. Sometimes, they're even forced to leave their homes, or they're put through so much hardship that they really have no choice but to leave—all to make room for new Israeli settlers.

They face police brutality: Israeli police routinely enter neighborhoods (like al-'Esawiyah) for no valid reason other than to do things like stop traffic, conduct inspections, verbally assault residents, randomly order shops to shut down, raid homes and search them without warrants, and falsely arrest minors (more on that in a bit). Police use the sometimes disruptive responses to justify even more of a police presence, and the cycle of abuses starts all over again.

Then there's the Israeli military, which kills, wounds, beats, and abuses countless Palestinians each year—again, oftentimes for no discernible reason.

And each year, hundreds of Palestinian minors are picked up on the street or at home in the middle of the night, handcuffed and blindfolded, and whisked off to be interrogated. Many are sleep-deprived and are given nothing to eat or drink for hours. They aren't allowed to consult with an adult or a lawyer. They deal with yelling, threats, verbal abuse, and sometimes physical violence. And oftentimes, these interrogations end with plea deals and arrests.

In April 2021, Human Rights Watch even released a (controversial) report declaring that the Israeli gov's treatment of Palestinians in the West Bank (think: illegal occupation and discrimination) amount to crimes against humanity of apartheid and persecution. You read that right.

Take a moment to let all that sink in: the systemic abuse of a group of people who are continually being ignored by the world. Even Palestinian leadership, especially Hamas, isn't doing much to help them.

Where do we go from here? Good question. By now, you've seen that plenty of people have tried (and failed) to work toward peace. It's made even trickier because both sides have victims and perpetrators, though an imbalance of power certainly exists. Here are the main few options for any sort of solution to this conflict.

TWO-STATE SOLUTION	ONE-STATE SOLUTION (Option A)	ONE-STATE SOLUTION (Option B)
An independent Israel and an independent Palestine would be formed.	Israel, the West Bank, and the Gaza Strip would get mashed together into one big country.	Israel, the West Bank, and the Gaza Strip would get mashed together into one big country.
Israel would be mostly run by (and for) Jews and Israelis; Palestine would be mostly run by and for Palestinians.	Israel would become a single democratic country where Arab Muslims coexist with Jews—and outnumber them.	Israel as it exists today would go ahead with annexing the West Bank and force out Palestinians . . . or deny them the right to vote.
The idea of a democratic Jewish state exists in this scenario, as does an independent Palestinian one.	The state remains a democracy and likely loses its Jewish nature in favor of a Palestinian one.	Israel remains a Jewish state but would no longer be a democracy.
This plan is favored by nearly everyone, especially the international community as a whole.	This plan is favored by some Israelis on the left—plus some Palestinians. But most people oppose a plan that would put an end to the only Jewish state in existence.	This plan is favored by some Israelis on the right. But much of the world—including the vast majority of Zionists—see the plan as a human rights violation.

There are a few big factors that complicate the implementation of any one of these solutions:

Hamas: Like I mentioned before, the group wants a Palestinian country . . . and absolutely does not want Israel to exist—putting them basically in the camp of Option A. And regardless of how many Palestinians share this view (hint: most don't), the fact of the matter is that Hamas controls the gov in Gaza . . .

The Palestinian Authority: This group controls the gov in the West Bank—meaning there's not even really one singular Palestinian gov that reps the entire people. The Palestinian Authority wants a two-state solution, and they've been spending the last decade or so working to build an independent state and a better future for Palestinians so that can become a reality. But ICYMI, those efforts are threatened by Israeli settlements.

Israel's gov: Even though Israelis don't have a divided govern-ment like Palestinians do, there are definitely right-wingers who would much prefer Option B of the one-state solution to any other scenario (but again: most don't).

The Israel-Palestine conflict in general is extremely complicated, and nuanced, and tangled. And it's pretty hard to get to the heart of it—or even begin getting there—without looking at the fullest pic-ture possible.

When you do, you'll see a knotted web of alliances and treaties and agreements. A pattern of just nearly reaching peace . . . before it all disappears in a wave of violence. A clash of views so opposing in every which way that it's hard not to feel like a solution of any sort is impossible.

But, news flash: it's possible.

Now here's what most people don't see.

Everything else. Or, for that matter, everyone else. Because if there's one thing most Palestinians and most Israelis have in common, it's that they want peace. They want an end to the fighting. The people who don't are a small—but extremely consequential—extreme.

Throughout all of history, there have been moments like this when peace feels out of the question.

It never really is.

You want to know why?

You exist. Yes, you. You have the power to break the pattern. You have the power to make peace something that's not only possible, but completely achievable.

We all do.

And then? Who knows where we can take the world.

9/11, the War in Afghanistan, and the Iraq War

Picture this:

You're walking down the street on a bright September morning. You're in New York City, and the sky is a brilliant cerulean. Thin wisps of clouds streak the sky as if airbrushed. Towering skyscrapers gleam in the cool sunlight.

You glance up, shielding your eyes with your hand.

You see a plane. It glides overhead, low.

You don't quite register what you're seeing. But you feel it. You feel it in the pit of your stomach.

Something is wrong.

Time begins to move differently. First, it goes slowly. You watch as the plane passes building after building after building. You watch as it veers toward the Twin Towers. You watch as it gets closer, closer.

Time speeds up.

The plane crashes.

All at once the world is filled with the sounds of screeching and screaming as the plane pierces the building.

Later, you'll look at pictures taken from afar. The plane looks so small, so innocent. It nearly seems as though it has been edited beside the hulking giants of the Twin Towers. The pictures don't line up with reality; in person, it is huge. The plane, the noise, the smoke, the debris. It seems like space is filled with far too much of anything. Reality is flooded.

You run.

You run away from the Twin Towers, but you no longer recognize where you're going. The sky, once bright and blue, is thick with smoke. This, too, seems to move outside the realm of time. The smoke hunts you, billowing from the plane in the building like a nuclear mushroom cloud and invading your lungs.

Suddenly, as if waking from a dream, you see a stampede of people running. Most of them are running in the same direction as you. But there are also countless firefighters running in the other direction.

By this time, people are watching across the country on TV. People are watching, and they're numb. Confused. They are in a state of shock.

And then they see something else in the sky.

Like the plane, this seems like something that just shouldn't be there, way up there in the sky. It seems impossibly small. But as the world keeps watching, it becomes increasingly apparent that this something is a person.

This is a person, throwing themselves from the building and hurtling toward the ground.

And they are not alone.

A collective jolt goes through the system of every American watching from their homes. And that jolt keeps twisting further and further into horror as they hear about another plane hitting the Twin Towers.

Then another plane, this time into the Pentagon.

Then another, now in Pennsylvania. (It will later be discovered that it was supposed to hit the White House, but passengers on board fought to regain control.)

And that's when the towers start to fall.

The sound is deafening. The Twin Towers groan and shriek. They don't go down without a fight.

But when they do go down, they fall hard.

A cloud of dust and debris adds to the oppressive smoke in the sky.

People who were there on September 11th battle with the trauma and the health effects to this day. The dust was made of pulverized concrete and construction debris and asbestos and even lead and mercury. It was wildly toxic. And eventually, it began causing cancer.

To this day, people—many of whom are firefighters and first responders—are continuing to die.

People who weren't there and watched from home were struck with a terror unlike anything else.

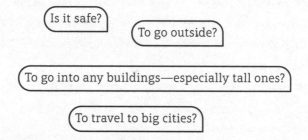

No one knew what was happening. All they knew was that it was an attack—the very first on the continental United States of America. And the very first attack on the United States in general since Pearl Harbor.

You probably know the story of 9/11. It's arguably one of the single most impactful moments in American history. 2,977 people were killed. Al-Qaeda, a terrorist group in the Middle East, was at fault.

And the US was forever changed. Ever been to an airport? Those kinds of security measures were intro'd as a result of 9/11. Think: the Transportation Security Administration (aka the TSA) and its parent agency, the Dept of Homeland Security (aka the DHS).

The country was also changed in some fundamental ways. Following 9/11, it was filled with a palpable fear, one that still looms over our political landscape today. Remember that rise in Islamophobia we talked about earlier on? This is one place where it started to come into play.

And the rest of the world? Well, that was perhaps affected just as significantly.

Afghanistan

Meet the Taliban.

If you haven't noticed yet, a lot of events I mention in this book come back into play in later chapters—and the war in Afghanistan is no different.

Case in point: like I mentioned in the Cold War chapter, the Soviet Union entered Afghanistan in 1979 to set up a communist gov (which meant the US was also hanging around in Afghanistan to fight the Soviets via proxies). But right around when the war was dying down in the 1980s, the Soviets began to ditch Afghanistan, making way for a new group to take charge: the Taliban.

The Taliban initially popped up in northern Pakistan, in religious seminaries (or theological/divinity schools) that were typically funded by Saudi Arabia. The majority-Pashtun (which is an ethnic group) movement preached a hardline version of Sunni Islam and pledged to bring peace, security, and their form of religion back to Pashtun areas in Pakistan and Afghanistan.

The group quickly expanded from there. By 1998, it controlled a full 90 percent of Afghanistan.

You read that right.

The Taliban was originally greeted with open arms by much of the Afghan population, who were weary of constant infighting since the Soviets left. But it didn't take long for the group to face some pushback. Hint: it intro'd or supported punishments like public executions of convicted murderers and adulterers and amputations for those found guilty of theft. Plus restrictions saying men needed to grow out beards and women needed to wear burkas. Girls aged ten and over weren't really allowed to go to school, and television, music, and movies were banned.

They also committed lots more human rights violations and cultural abuses.

And here's a key thing to know: the Taliban didn't get to having that much power on its own. It was aided by a powerful ally: al-Qaeda.

Before I get into that alliance, here are the deets on al-Qaeda. Like the Taliban, al-Qaeda was able to build power because of the Soviet Union's invasion of Afghanistan. During that invasion, a Muslim insurgency (or rebellion) bent on fighting a jihad (or holy war—a war waged to support Islam or another cause) against the Soviets started taking shape. One of the leaders of that insurgency was **Osama bin Laden**, who offered up money, weapons, and fighters. He soon got in touch with other insurgents, who put together a large financial network—a network that ultimately shifted into al-Qaeda once the Soviets ditched Afghanistan.

Al-Qaeda's goal? Expel the US from what they considered Muslim lands by fighting holy wars whenever—and wherever—they popped up. Led by Osama bin Laden, the group set up shop throughout the Middle East and declared a holy war on the United States . . . Jews . . . and their allies.

In the following years, they carried out a number of terror attacks.

Including 9/11.

But for all that al-Qaeda came into being around the same time as the Taliban, and for all that they helped each other out, the two groups had some pretty big differences.

ICYMI, the Taliban sort of operated like a gov. They were often violent and brutal, but there was also this sense of broad organization. They were trying to administer a state. Compare that to al-Qaeda, which was really more of a rogue terrorist group with a much smaller and much more hidden presence—until they struck. They basically operated as a small underground army.

The Taliban and al-Qaeda crossed paths often. In the 1990s, the Taliban even asked al-Qaeda for money. That relationship eventually grew to a full-scale alliance that literally still exists today. And the Taliban's role in that alliance was largely that of the protector.

Long story short: it didn't take long for people to realize al-Qaeda was hiding out with the Taliban in Afghanistan following 9/11. And not only that, but some of the terrorists involved in 9/11 had even trained there.

So you can see why all eyes were on Afghanistan in October 2001.

PHASE ONE

Bush Announces Opening of Attacks (CNN)

Bush Announces Strike against Taliban
(*The Washington Post*)

A Nation Challenged: The Attack; US and Britain Strike Afghanistan, Aiming at Bases and Terrorist Camps; Bush Warns "Taliban Will Pay a Price" (*The New York Times*)

The United States' mission to hunt down those responsible for 9/11—al-Qaeda—quickly turned into a broader attack on the Taliban. Not only did the US want to find Osama bin Laden and make him pay, they also wanted to drive out the Taliban for good.

It didn't start out that way. The US first reached out to the Taliban's leader, Mullah Mohammed Omar, and pretty much demanded that they hand over "all the leaders of al-Qaeda" (as Bush said) who were hanging out in Afghanistan. To which Omar said, *That's a no.*

So the US—with the help of the British and anti-Taliban allies in Afghanistan—carried out a plan for war. They were also aided by the Northern Alliance, a coalition of militias that still had control over a very, very small part of Afghanistan.

Afghanistan

Northern Alliance

Anti-Taliban Guerrilla Operations

Taliban

The war's public start was October 7, 2001—not even a month after 9/11 took place. US and British warplanes went after Taliban targets, with the Northern Alliance seizing towns that had previously been held by the Taliban. (For the record, the Northern Alliance's relationship with the US wasn't always all that great. Even after the Taliban retreated, the Northern Alliance ignored the US's advice and took the capital of Kabul.)

On December 6, southern Afghanistan's largest city, Kandahar, fell to the Northern Alliance (this one was on the US's terms).

It was the end of Taliban political power.

For now.

What followed was an all-out manhunt for Osama bin Laden.

And here's the thing: the US almost had him. Or at least that's what everyone now thinks (hindsight is 20/20, right?). But just as the US attacked his mountain stronghold in December 2001, he (supposedly) snuck off into Abbottabad, Pakistan.

That became al-Qaeda's new base. And the battle made its way over there, too. In March 2002, US and Afghan forces fought about eight hundred al-Qaeda and Taliban militants. Historic, BTW. See: for the first time in the Afghanistan war, troops from Australia, Canada, Denmark, France, Germany, and Norway joined in.

That's largely thought to be the end of phase one—which lasted a grand total of two months—of this war.

But phase two was just getting started.

And thiiiiiis one wasn't nearly as quick.

Not even close.

PHASE TWO

Over the years, the US has faced a lot of criticism about its tendency to, you know, invade a country, fight a war, and then leave it totally unstable and in all kinds of crises. (I'll let you decide whether you think that criticism is valid as you read on.)

So they really didn't want to deal with that kind of backlash again in Afghanistan.

Enter: phase two of the war, which saw the US—and the international community as a whole—working to rebuild Afghanistan now that the Taliban was gone (again . . . for now).

In theory, this was pretty straightforward. But only in theory.

Between 2001 and 2009, the US Congress handed about $38 billion in humanitarian and reconstruction assistance to Afghanistan.

Much of it went to training Afghan security forces to keep the Taliban and al-Qaeda from popping up again. The rest of it wasn't nearly enough to completely develop Afghanistan—plus there was a whole lot of confusion over where responsibility for leading things like education, health, and agriculture lay. It gets worse: all that funding was plagued by things like corruption, inefficiencies, and dysfunction. You want to know where a whole lot of that money ended up going? To American bizes and contractors.

Then there was the matter of elections. At first, things seemed to be going pretty well, with about 80 percent voter turnout for the 2004 Afghan elections—the first since the fall of the Taliban. But the gov soon faced serious issues of corruption.

This, coupled with the US's agonizingly slow attempts at reconstruction, started turning public opinion against Westerners.

That's when everything really went downhill.

Starting in 2005, the Taliban made a comeback. Except this time, it used methods more typically seen of terrorist groups. Think: suicide bombings, buried bombs . . . you get the idea. As the months went on, violence and death at the hands of the Taliban soared.

So did public dissent against the US—even more so than before. In 2006, a US military vehicle crashed and killed multiple Afghans, sparking massive anti-American riots in Kabul.

This was a big turning point. The riots prompted the US to step back—and NATO to step in and really take command of the war. (They first got involved in 2003, but this was when they really ramped it up.)

But the US only really stepped back publicly. Secretly, they were carrying out targeted killings of Taliban leaders.

This basically brings us to the end of phase two of the war. It lasted about seven or eight years. To sum things up: US reconstruction efforts? Fail. Attempts to keep the Taliban from making a resurgence? Big fail.

PHASE THREE

The end of phase two of the War in Afghanistan came and went without anyone really realizing it. But when phase three hit, it was undeniable that things were escalating in a way that they hadn't in many, many years.

So, it's 2008. Barack Obama wins the presidency. He pledges to spotlight the War in Afghanistan.

And spotlight it he does.

Just months after being elected, he sent an additional seventeen thousand troops to Afghanistan, adding to the thirty-six thousand already there—not to mention thirty-two thousand NATO service members. The goal? Protect the Afghan population from further attacks, and prevent the Taliban from getting too established. Again.

Since this was the goal, not a lot of attention was given to trying to kill militants. Instead, US troops tried to sway enemy fighters to their side and tried to get Taliban leaders to make peace with Afghanistan's gov.

This plan was all well and good, except for one major flaw: there weren't enough US troops in Afghanistan to make it a reality. It soon came out that the US would decisively and conclusively lose the War in Afghanistan . . . unless a looooot more troops were sent there.

And that's precisely what happened. Another thirty thousand troops were deployed to Afghanistan by the summer of 2010. And as the number of troops upped, so did the number of deaths.

What else increased during this time: US drone strikes—specifically in Pakistan.

In the following months, a lot happened—and a lot didn't. The US fought battles, gave the Afghan gov a stern talking-to about its corruption and fraud problems, and tried to get the Taliban and the Afghan gov to get along. None of those things ultimately accomplished much.

TEN YEARS SINCE THE START OF THE WAR

Let's refocus a bit. Quick refresher: this whole war started because of 9/11. Because the US was trying to kill Osama bin Laden and take down al-Qaeda for good. And all this time, those efforts went on.

But those efforts started to intensify even more in 2011. The US—and basically the whole world—was getting tired of what was starting to feel like an endless war in Afghanistan, especially since it wasn't really going anywhere. Everyone wanted to get out as fast as possible.

So when it was finally discovered where Osama bin Laden had been hiding all this time—and US forces killed him in a raid in 2011—the US did just that (sort of). But the process definitely wasn't fast.

Over the course of 2011, security controls were gradually handed back to the Afghan military and police. Instead of relying on US troops for defense, for the first time in years, that burden began to be shouldered by Afghanistan.

It didn't work. Civilian casualties and insurgent attacks were still very high.

And from there, it actually got even worse.

In 2012, a video surfaced showing US Marines urinating on dead Afghans. Not long after that, it came out that US soldiers had burned copies of the Koran at a military base. A month after *that*, a US soldier allegedly broke into multiple Afghan homes and shot and killed sixteen people. Massive riots and protests followed, but even more significant was the fact that the Taliban halted peace talks with the US and the Afghan gov.

NATO wasn't having much luck, either. They were attempting to train Afghan soldiers and police, some of whom were turning their weapons right back on NATO soldiers.

Either way, the US was determined to leave Afghanistan. So the two countries sat down and agreed on a list of terms—one of which involved letting Afghan forces handle night raids on Taliban leaders.

So fast-forward to 2014. The US and NATO's combat mission in Afghanistan formally ended. What didn't end: US military presence in Afghanistan. But for the first time in a while, it *was* decreasing.

2001:	2,500 troops
2002:	9,700
2003:	13,100
2004:	20,300
2005:	holds steady at about 20,000
2006:	holds steady at about 20,000
2007:	25,000
2008:	32,500
2009:	67,000
2010:	100,000
2011:	90,000
2012:	77,000
2013:	46,000
2014:	16,100
2015:	9,800
2016:	8,400

And then, on February 29, 2020, it happened. The beginning of the end:

Afghan Conflict: US and Taliban Sign Deal to End 18-Year War (BBC)

U.S. Signs a Peace Deal with the Taliban, but Is the War in Afghanistan Really Ending? (NBC News)

And over the next bunch of months—through the summer and fall of 2021—it continued:

Biden announces U.S. military mission in Afghanistan will end August 31 (CBS News)

U.S. military official says a 'complete Taliban takeover' is possible in Afghanistan (NYT)

Taliban enter Afghan capital as US diplomats evacuate by chopper (Reuters)

U.S. ends 20-year war in Afghanistan with final evacuation flights out of Kabul (CNBC)

Afghan women fear 'dark' future, loss of rights as Taliban seize control (NBC News)

Terrorism will increase under Afghanistan's newly appointed Taliban government, experts warn (CNBC)

20-Year U.S. War Ending as It Began, With Taliban Ruling Afghanistan (NYT)

While this marked the end of the war in Afghanistan for the US, it marked the start of a whole new phase of suffering and crisis for Afghans, especially Afghan women.

It's hard not to wonder where the country will go from here.

And it's hard not to wonder whether anything was accomplished at all.

The fact of the matter is, the US entered Afghanistan to prevent it from becoming a safe haven for terrorists and to kill Osama bin Laden. And, yes—they did accomplish the latter (the former is still kind of up in the air, especially with the Taliban's return).

But what happened in Afghanistan as the US tried (and failed) to democratize and redevelop it became more of a focus of the war than anyone had ever anticipated.

Just sit on that for a few minutes.

Iraq War

Afghanistan's not the only major war that resulted from 9/11.

You guessed it: Iraq.

I'll start off by saying that like the War in Afghanistan there's a lot of debate over the necessity of the Iraq War. But unlike Afghanistan, that debate was taking place even before US troops first set foot in Iraq.

Picture this. It's 2002. George W. Bush is the US's prez. 9/11 is fresh in Americans' minds. The country feels vulnerable.

There's a laser focus on the Middle East as a whole, largely because of al-Qaeda. That focus landed on Iraq.

That's right—in 2002, Prez Bush stated that Iraq was harboring "weapons of mass destruction," and not only that, but it was continuing to build them. (Many people disputed this, however.)

Add that to the fact that Bush pointed fingers at Iraq for allegedly supporting al-Qaeda, and the US was ready to head to war.

The apparent reasons didn't end there.

Meet Saddam Hussein. He was Iraq's prez. And he was very unpopular in the US.

Back it up: in the early 1990s, the US fought a relatively quick war known as the Gulf War. The reason? Hussein was hell-bent on boosting Iraq's economy . . . so he invaded the neighboring country of Kuwait to take control of its oil fields.

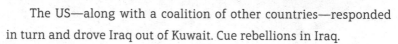

The US—along with a coalition of other countries—responded in turn and drove Iraq out of Kuwait. Cue rebellions in Iraq.

Hussein's reaction was fast and harsh. Thousands of people were murdered. Others seemingly vanished into Iraq's prison system. Still others were forced to flee to refugee camps.

After the Gulf War, the United Nations struck a ceasefire with Iraq that basically mandated that the country couldn't produce or possess chemical, biological, or nuclear weapons (this is important).

Only a slight problem . . . Iraq wasn't exactly complying with UN arms inspectors.

That brings us back to 2002. Like I said—the US is kind of freaking out about the idea that Iraq might have nuclear weapons. The UN basically tells the US to calm down . . . and passes a resolution demanding Iraq let inspectors come take a look at whether they're actually holding up their end of the ceasefire terms.

Here's where things get tricky.

At this point, the US and the UK think Iraq ignored the resolution. Much of the United Nations—including France and Germany—believe otherwise. And actually advocate to give Iraq more time to comply with the inspections.

But it's the breaking point for the US. In 2003, they gave Saddam an ultimatum: get out of Iraq within forty-eight hours, or else.

France: QUELS IMBÉCILES! WHAT DID YOU JUST DO?????

US: take a chill pill. i took care of things.

France: EVEN RUSSIA THINKS THIS IS A BAD IDEA. AND THEY'RE RUSSIA!

Russia: yup.

Germany: nein nein nein nein nein. don't do this, america.

France: EARTH TO THE US. ARE YOU HEARING US?

Germany: i don't like this, america. do you understand where you're going?

US: uh . . . yeah. to war. duh.

Maybe it didn't go exactly like that. But the point is: pretty much no one thought the Iraq War was a good idea. And it hadn't even gotten started yet.

But that didn't stop the US.

PHASE ONE

It probably comes as no surprise that Saddam Hussein totally did not listen to the US's ultimatum.

US Invasion of Iraq "Inevitable" (BBC)

Bush Sends Iraq War Letter to Congress (CNN)

Threats and Responses: The White House; Bush Orders Start of War on Iraq; Missiles Apparently Miss Hussein
(*The New York Times*)

So . . . that happened.

The war itself was brief. Between March and April of 2003, forces from the US and the UK—plus some smaller contingents from other countries—invaded Iraq. Iraq's military was no match. In fact, some forces just retreated before a battle could even be fought.

Eventually, nearly every big city had been taken by US forces and allies. On May 1, the US declared an end to major combat operations.

SIX MONTHS LATER . . .

. . . Saddam Hussein was captured.

Yes, really. And six months from then? The US turned him over to Iraqi authorities. He stood trial for a long list of crimes. He was convicted of crimes against humanity.

He was executed on December 30, 2006.

If that all seems like it moved pretty quickly, it's because it did.

But the impact of these few months of war was cataclysmic.

PHASE TWO

Once Saddam Hussein's regime collapsed, it didn't take long for discord to spread throughout Iraq. There was a widespread wave of looting and violence—violence that soon set its sights on US forces in a big way.

Like in Afghanistan, the US invading Iraq completely destabilized it politically and economically, so much so that it actually kind of led to a civil war. To be super clear: Prez Bush and his team never ever described it that way, instead opting for the term "sectarian violence."

But the resulting deaths were never in doubt, with thousands of American soldiers dying in Iraq over the next couple years. Meanwhile, it's never been confirmed how many Iraqis died, but from the war's start to finish, it's been estimated that as many as 308,000 were killed.

This sort of violence went on and on and on.

Here's another similarity to Afghanistan. While there was huge opposition to the Iraq War right from the start (millions marched in antiwar rallies), as time went on, even more Americans began to turn against the war.

And here's why.

Turns out . . . there were never any weapons of mass destruction in Iraq. None. Zip. Zilch. Nada.

And turns out . . . there wasn't really any evidence that Iraq had supported al-Qaeda.

So then . . . why?

Why did the US invade Iraq? Start a war that killed hundreds of thousands of people? Further destabilize not only Iraq, but arguably the Middle East as a whole?

You're not the only one wondering. Many Americans were asking that during the war, too.

And I wish I could answer. But the fact of the matter is, to this day, no one really knows for sure.

Maybe it was for the same reasons Saddam Hussein invaded Kuwait all those years ago: Oil. Money. Iraq certainly had a lot of oil, and since the war, lots of Western oil bizes (think: ExxonMobil, Chevron, BP, Shell . . . to name a few) have made it big there in a way that they couldn't have before, since they very literally weren't allowed to. They weren't the only ones to benefit.

American oil service bizes found financial success in Iraq, too. Incluuuuuuding Halliburton. Sound familiar? Probably because Prez Bush's running mate, Dick Cheney, led the Texas-based biz before becoming vice prez. There's even speculation that the US knew there were never weapons of mass destruction in Iraq, and made it all up—or, at least, greatly exaggerated the situation—just to get the American public to support the war. Unconfirmed, BTW.

That's the enduring theory. But it's not the only one.

Regardless of the reason, the US had now entered a war they couldn't so easily leave. It wasn't until 2011 when, after years of increasing and decreasing troops and continuous violence and lots of negotiations, the US formally completed its withdrawal of troops from Iraq (although a few thousand US troops are still there).

So that's the Iraq War. Controversial from birth to death.

And perhaps even after death.

Because the results of the Iraq War are much more far-reaching than first appears.

Like I've hinted at throughout this whole entire section, war isn't just something that takes place between two govs in a vacuum. The citizens of every country involved are always watching. Always reacting. Always forming opinions, perspectives, prejudices.

Always suffering. Deeply, deeply suffering.

War is divide. Fundamentally, it is born of divide. But what's often forgotten is the divide it continues to create.

The fact of the matter is, the US went to war in Iraq. Countless lives were impacted by that. Iraqi lives. American lives. And people don't easily forget that.

Islamophobia continued to skyrocket in the United States. Distrust of Muslims and Middle Easterners was rampant. And that feeling was mutual among many Iraqis.

To many Iraqis, the US was needlessly and selfishly wrecking lives. It was the antagonist. The enemy. The wrongdoer.

The division of war led to hate, and that hate led to new violence and new wars.

I'm talking about ISIS.

You've probably grown up hearing about ISIS, so I won't get into it too much. But I will say that it's a brutal terrorist group that spread fear and violence across Iraq. And while it was technically created in 1999, it only rose to prominence and began participating in the Iraqi insurgency after the US invaded Iraq in 2003. And it gained even more power because of the vacuum left by the US pullback.

So I'll end the Iraq War discussion by saying this: even though the war is over, the effects . . . are most definitely not.

Who knows if they'll ever truly be?

Okay. So let's expand this a bit and look back on this section as a whole. The Wars. You may have picked up on a pattern—of war, of violence and death, of growing public dissent, of withdrawal. And even though public dissent isn't physically part of the wars themselves, it's a key component here. Because, who knows? If people didn't take it upon themselves to pay serious attention to what was going on in these wars—from Vietnam to Iraq—maybe we'd still be in them. (And in some cases, we are still in them, which is why it's all the more crucial for us to inform ourselves so we have the power to do some public dissenting.)

We can cause wars. But we can also end them.

It may sound simple, but that way of thinking extends to, well, everything.

Turn the page. You'll see what I mean.

THE MOVEMENTS

History is made up of a series of movements.

The rising and falling of empires, the progressing of civilization, the gaining and eroding of human rights. The world is constantly playing a game of tug-of-war—except it's really about the furthest thing from a game.

But while we're at it, let's keep using this metaphor of tug-of-war. The rules of tug-of-war are usually pretty simple. There are two sides and one rope.

However, in the case of the movements we're about to dive into (plus so many more that we just don't have room to cover here), one side of the rope is a foot thick, with handles to grab on to. This is the side of the people in power. These people have basically always been in power, so they've had centuries to build up the rope and give themselves an advantage in this game of tug-of-war. These people in power have their idea of how things should work, and they don't want anyone to get in the way of that.

On the other side, the rope is not much more than a string. This is the side of literally everyone else. These people have never had the kind of control that the people in power have. Their side of the rope is wearing down. The edges are twisted and frayed. The rope is thiiiiis close to snapping.

Three kinds of people exist on this side of the rope. There are those who see only how frayed the rope is and think the best way to do things is to tread carefully. They tug the rope slowly, inching toward more rights, more control, more of whatever it is that their movement is aiming to change. Usually, the people in power are okay with this. Maybe they even give up those few precious inches of rope willingly, because they're much more afraid of the next group of people.

These people see the rope as something that shouldn't even be there in the first place. *Why should just a few select people have power?* they ask. They want to get rid of the rope and replace it with some other kind of system that allows them to have more equity, more justice, more balance.

Finally, there are those who love the rope and love the people in power. Lots of these people share certain attributes with the people in power, and because of this, they're given special privileges. They're totally happy with the way things are. Since this game of tug-of-war works so well for them, they're convinced that the other two groups on their side of the rope will only ever make things worse. When those who believe in slowly pulling the rope try to inch toward more balance, they knock them over. And when those who believe in replacing the rope with a new system try to fight for what they want, those who love the rope fight, too—but against them.

This delicate balance has existed throughout all of history.

What you're about to read will take you through the times that the rope has come closer and closer to being destroyed.

Where do you stand? Which group do you fall into? Try to ask yourself that as you begin reading. Try to see yourself in these movements—because in most cases, they're far from over.

Women's Suffrage

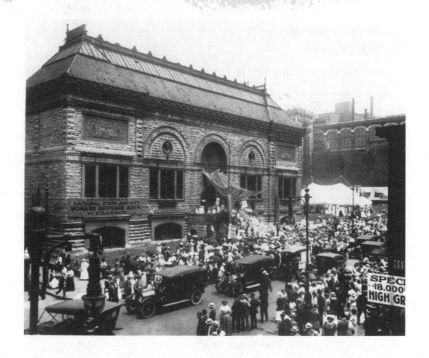

Chances are you've heard a whole lot about feminism. Maybe you've heard people talk about reproductive rights or the gender pay gap. Or maybe you've had conversations about rape culture or the lack of female representation in far too many institutions. The point is: modern-day feminism is a very, very big movement.

But I'm not here to talk about that. I'm here to talk about where this all started—and where the modern-day idea of women's rights protests started gaining steam in the first place.

Let's head back in time: The year is 1848. The setting? Seneca Falls, New York.

We hold these truths to be self-evident: that all men and women are created equal . . .

Sound different?

That's the point.

In case you haven't figured it out yet, we're at the Seneca Falls Convention—considered to be the start of the women's rights movement. While women's rights were already a topic of conversation at the time (but not nearly as much as they should've been, honestly), this was the very first women's rights convention in the United States. Almost two hundred women showed up.

But let's keep listening.

The history of mankind is a history of repeated injuries and usurpations on the part of man toward woman, having in direct object the establishment of an absolute tyranny over her. To prove this, let facts be submitted to a candid world.

He has never permitted her to exercise her inalienable right to the elective franchise.

He has compelled her to submit to laws, in the formation of which she had no voice . . .

He has made her, if married, in the eye of the law, civilly dead.

He has taken from her all right in property, even to the wages she earns . . .

He closes against her all the avenues to wealth and distinction, which he considers most honorable to himself. As a teacher of theology, medicine, or law, she is not known.

He has denied her the facilities for obtaining a thorough education—all colleges being closed against her.

He has endeavored, in every way that he could, to destroy her confidence in her own powers, to lessen her self-respect, and to make her willing to lead a dependent and abject life . . .

Now, in view of this entire disfranchisement of one-half the people of this country, their social and religious degradation,—in view of the unjust laws above mentioned, and because women do feel themselves aggrieved, oppressed, and fraudulently deprived of their most sacred rights, we insist that they have immediate admission to all the rights and privileges which belong to them as citizens of the United States.

Pretty powerful stuff, especially for that time. And that was just the beginning. Over the coming decades, women's rights activists continued to educate people about the validity of the movement.

These women might not have had the full support of the general public yet—but they did have petitions. And with these petitions, they worked to lobby Congress to pass a constitutional amendment to enfranchise women. In other words: give women the same privileges afforded any other citizen. Or, you know, any other white man. (Black men got the right to vote in 1870, but they still had way more hurdles to voting than white men.)

Only a slight problem . . . few lawmakers actually paid any attention. Hardly any men at the time—particularly the men in gov—seemed to think women deserved those same privileges. Which is right about when women's rights activists realized what they needed to focus on in particular.

The right to vote.

These activists figured that if existing lawmakers weren't going to fight for their rights, they needed to vote those guys out—and vote in people who actually cared about women's rights. But first, they needed to get that important right to vote—aka suffrage.

A lot of influential figures emerged in this fight, but ultimately,

 it came down to two main groups employing two main tactics.

Spoiler alert: it helps to think of these two tactics through the lens of sexism—or, more specifically, as different approaches to all the hurdles raised by sexism.

First up: the National American Woman Suffrage Association (aka NAWSA), which was created in 1890 and led by women like Elizabeth Cady Stanton and Susan B. Anthony. Its goal was pretty straightforward: recruit more women (specifically college-educated, privileged, and politically influential women), petition and lobby individual states to let women vote, and, hopefully, use this to pressure Congress into passing a constitutional amendment and federal law expanding voting rights to include women.

But that doesn't really even begin to cover the massive importance of NAWSA. I'll put it like this: there is no American women's suffrage movement without NAWSA. The movement was largely coordinated by NAWSA, and with the help of statewide and local chapters, its influence grew rapidly.

NAWSA was extra political and extra diplomatic. Remember that tug-of-war analogy? The women of NAWSA were the people slowly pulling the rope and working angles to get the people in power to give them what they wanted. One of the most significant examples of this came right around World War I, when NAWSA encouraged women to help out with war efforts.

That did a lot of things. It helped recognize the reality of the working American woman. It then underscored the value of women. And it gave people even more reasons to cheer for women.

Whiiiich gave the gov no choice but to acknowledge the women's suffrage movement and pay attention to their demands.

Back to that in a second.

Not everyone in the women's suffrage movement was a fan of NAWSA. Society at the time (and, let's be honest, society today) mandated that women needed to be polite. Kind. Gentle. Meek. You could maybe argue that NAWSA was very aware of this, and that's why they took such a nonaggressive and diplomatic route, but there were other women at the time who felt that in doing so, they were playing right into all that existing sexism, or they were compromising their values. Like, why should women be polite and gentle to the very same people who had thus far denied them rights?

Enter: the National Women's Party (aka NWP), which formed in 1913. It was basically the exact opposite of NAWSA in every aspect other than, you know, trying to get women the right to vote. They were the people who wanted to take a big giant ax to the rope.

And they certainly tried.

Some key differences between the two suffrage groups: unlike NAWSA, which tried to work with politicians to change policy, the NWP disliked literally every single member of the Democrat Party—the party in power at the time—regardless of their individual stances on women's rights. Because, accountability. Their strategy was to skip the state and local channels and go straight to the root of the problem and get things changed on a federal level.

For some context, women's suffrage was already a very big topic of conversation in Britain—with "militant," "radical," "extremist" suffragists often leading the way. (You'll get why those quotes are there in a second.) The NWP kind of modeled its methods on those British suffragists.

In 1913, Alice Paul and Lucy Burns—who were part of NAWSA at the time, but broke away to form the NWP almost three years later—organized a parade advocating for women's rights. In response, antisuffrage riots broke out in Washington, DC. Over the next three years, the NWP kept on organizing more protests, pickets, and parades to raise awareness about women's suffrage.

In many instances, suffragists who picketed at the White House were arrested and fined for blocking traffic. They shook their heads to paying the fine and were quickly taken away to a jail, where they went on a hunger strike and were subsequently force-fed through a tube by officials. That's literally torture.

So yeah. That's what defined "militant" suffragists. Protesting. Picketing. Parading. Basically, fighting for the right to vote publicly and visibly, from the outside, as opposed to politely and from within the existing systems of power, like NAWSA did. (But don't be mistaken: the NWP also had a super-sophisticated lobbying operation that worked within the gov and was backed up by their ability to get the attention of the general public.)

If you're anything like me, you're probably thinking that dubbing that as "militant" does sound a liiiiiiittle bit harsh. It's definitely not on par with today's definition of militant. Maybe it came down to the fact that those in power were threatened by women standing up and fighting for their rights, even if "fighting" was usually something fairly peaceful, like marching down a street and holding up signs. But regardless, even NAWSA was opposed to the NWP's tactics. Yes, really.

That wasn't the only problem in the women's suffrage movement. Here's another: the movement was largely white. And while activists like Elizabeth Cady Stanton and Susan B. Anthony were vocally against slavery before the Civil War—and even found allies in abolitionists like Frederick Douglass—they became a little less vocal once it became clear that Black men would get the right to vote before white women. To which some white women said, *Well, that's degrading.*

Yeah. Big sigh.

What was even worse about the whole thing was that Black women obviously found it very degrading as well, but the political establishment expertly pitted Black and white women against each other and convinced the country that it could only handle one big reform at a time. (Society: Dividing Women Since I-Can't-Even-Count-How-Long.)

Oh, and here's another reason to sigh: like everything at the time, chapters of NAWSA and the NWP could be pretty segregated, and in some protests, Black women were forced to march separately.

As a result, Black suffragists have been pretty much erased from history. That's a problem—one that needs to be fixed.

Here are some prominent Black suffragists you need to know about. Keep in mind that these women are definitely not the *only* Black suffragists, so I encourage you to read up on others outside of this book.

First up: **Mary Church Terrell**. She was the prez of the National Association of Colored Women, which was founded in 1896 and aided women and kids suffering from things like health problems or a lack of education, housing, or clothing. She was also one of the first women to get a college degree. Then there was **Nannie Helen Boroughs**, who founded the National Training School for Women and Girls (now known as the Nannie Helen Boroughs School) in Washington, DC. And last but definitely not least: **Frances Ellen Watkins Harper**, who was an author, poet, essayist, abolitionist, and suffragist who became one of the first Black women to be published in the US.

Despite the racism involved, and despite the differences between NAWSA and NWP, all of the above were totally instrumental in the women's suffrage movement.

Okay. So we just established the two main groups and a few key figures in the women's suffrage movement. You can probably imagine they had their work cut out for them. Trying to get women the right to vote meant trying to add a new amendment (the Nineteenth Amendment) to the Constitution—something that (surprise surprise) is very, very hard to do. There are countless steps.

First: two-thirds of each chamber of Congress (the House of Representatives and the Senate) has to give the amendment the thumbs-up. The House of Reps had tried to pass the Nineteenth Amendment twice before, but both times, the Senate was a no-go. That was a pretty big pattern for this amendment. Since it was first intro'd in 1878, Congress as a whole had voted it down twenty-eight times. Not a typo. It wasn't until 1919 when Congress greenlighted it—and by just two votes.

Next: three-fourths of US states have to ratify the amendment. At the time, Alaska and Hawaii weren't states, so that meant suffragists had to get the approval of thirty-six states.

That's right—after countless decades of trying to convince Congress that women deserve the right to vote (can you imagine?), suffragists then had to go convince each individual US state of that same fact. (Or at least thirty-six of them.)

And not every state was that easy to convince. Some states flatout rejected the Nineteenth Amendment. In fact, it took another fourteen or so months of fighting, of state-by-state campaigns, and of a huge amount of effort on the part of the suffragists before the thirty-sixth state finally ratified it.

Last but not least: the US secretary of state has to certify the Nineteenth Amendment to the Constitution.

And in 1920, that very thing took place.

To be clear: while women did gain the right to vote in 1920, that mostly just applied to white women. Because even though the Nineteenth Amendment trashed the idea of using sex as a criteria for voting, it was undermined by aaaall the state laws in place that still made it a million billion times harder for citizens of color to vote (and the amendment didn't even cover Native American or Asian American women, who weren't considered citizens at the time).

Still, the Nineteenth Amendment was a very big deal. It was the single largest extension of voting rights in US history. And it was achieved through democratic processes. I'll repeat: petitioning, lobbying, protesting . . . you get the gist.

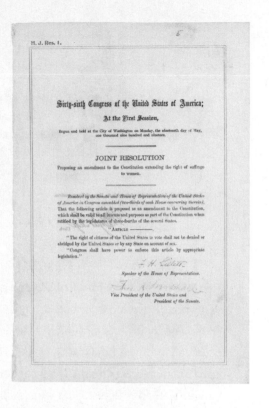

And, hey! Would you look at that. We still do all those things today to get laws passed and change made. In fact, all these tactics are used to continue advocating for women's rights, whether it's the Women's March or Me Too (but more on that really, really soon).

In case I haven't made my point yet:

After the Nineteenth Amendment, there was no doubt. Activism worked—and it would continue to work for decades to come.

The Hippie Movement

Now let's time-travel forward a few decades to the 1960s. The Vietnam War is raging. Lyndon B. Johnson is prez. The Beatles are literally everywhere. The civil rights movement is underway. The world just saw the construction of the Berlin Wall and the escalation and de-escalation of the Cuban Missile Crisis. TV journalism is becoming an increasingly popular method of figuring out what's going on in the world.

It may not seem like it, but these things were the perfect ingredients for a youth counterculture movement the likes of which had been never seen before.

Suspense, thick.

It all started with the Vietnam War. At first, it wasn't exactly the kind of thing that Americans were particularly concerned with. But in 1965, about a decade after the official start of the war, Prez Johnson deployed an additional fifty thousand ground troops to Vietnam.

And then there was the draft.

Aka when the gov basically holds a lottery for war—except this is one lottery you don't want to win. When the US gov passes legislation to enact a draft, you'd better hope either you're not eligible or your birthdate just doesn't get picked. Otherwise, you pretty much have no (legal) choice but to go to war.

U.S. Draft Call Doubled (UPI)

Cue instant uproar. You read about the Vietnam War a few chapters ago, so you know how this goes: the US loses. And as time went on and more blood was spilled, there was this growing sense in the US that Johnson was basically just sending these drafted men (many of whom were pretty young—late teens and early twenties) to their funerals.

People were losing their lives, their brothers, their sons, their husbands, their friends, all to a war that nobody really knew why the US was fighting.

And the worst part? People knew far more of the specifics about this war than any other before. Like I mentioned before, TV journalism was on the rise, which gave people a much closer and much more devastating look at the war. Before, wars could be fought and the gory deets wouldn't really be revealed until long after.

Thanks to TV journalism, the Vietnam War was very much the opposite.

That's a good thing, of course. It's important to be informed about what's going on, especially if it concerns something like war. But seeing and knowing the appalling things that happen during a war—seeing and knowing that your friends and family are facing such unspeakable things—that is nothing short of horrifying.

And people weren't going to ignore it.

"Hey, hey, LBJ, how many kids did you kill today?"

LBJ = Lyndon B. Johnson. And that chant (which is often still used at protests in various altered forms today, BTW) was just the beginning.

Because experiencing a war like that—whether you're learning about it from home or living it on the front lines—changes you.

It changes a generation.

Enter: the hippies.

I'll point out again how a lot of the people who were drafted for the Vietnam War were relatively young. That especially enraged college students, who were able to avoid being drafted but were furious at what was happening. And they weren't just furious with the war itself—they were furious with the US gov as a whole. That expanded into being disillusioned with ideas of materialism and repression.

In other words: a growing number of young people weren't exactly fans of the idea of prioritizing and favoring material goods over spirituality, or the idea of being chained down to a singular societal ideal.

They were over the gov, they were over institutions of power, and they were over social constructs.

While the hippies themselves actually didn't do very much protesting, they helped popularize an environment where young people felt powerful. Where young people felt like their voices mattered. Where young people felt united. Where young people felt like they could change the world.

That environment was further cultivated by things like music (with songs like "What's Going On" and "Imagine," which put into words what so many young people were feeling at the time), events

(in particular Woodstock and the Summer of Love, which both saw the celebration of peace and love on a massive scale), and organizations (including the Black Panthers, the Diggers, and Students for a

Democratic Society, all of which were early and incredibly important forms of youth activism).

And I'll remind you: all this was taking place amid the civil rights movement (more on that in just a few pages). Plus what was arguably the height of the Cold War. Not to mention greater protests for LGBTQ+ rights (more on this coming up soon, too).

It was a lot.

This convergence of events left some people feeling frightened or outraged or wronged. All those feelings funneled into one of the greatest periods of protest in recent US history—and it's still influencing us today.

In fact, you could maybe make a case for what's happening right this very instant—this rise of youth activism that's been taking place over the past few years—being the 1960s youth counterculture movement, part two.

And this time, we get to be a part of it.

The Civil Rights Movement

When you think of the civil rights movement, what or who do you think of?

Martin Luther King Jr.? His "I Have a Dream" speech?

Malcom X?

Ruby Bridges?

Segregation?

Emmett Till?

John Lewis?

All of the above are extremely important parts of the civil rights movement. And you'll definitely hear more about those people and those events in this chapter. But the actual story of the civil rights movement is much more complex.

I'll fill you in.

The Perilous Road to Civil Rights

The civil rights movement—which hit its peak in the '60s—spanned decades. By the time the movement truly launched in 1955, civil rights had been a big topic of discussion for many years. Jim Crow laws—which were a group of state and local policies that made racial segregation and discrimination legal—were widespread, and the Ku Klux Klan's reign of terror was in full swing. But at the same time, some progress was being made. In 1948, racial segregation in the armed forces legally ended. And in 1954, racial segregation in public schools legally ended (although lots of schools remained segregated).

Our story starts about a year later, in 1955. And it bears striking similarities to the Black Lives Matter movement (but more on that real soon).

1955

Meet Emmett Till. He was a fourteen-year-old Black youth who grew up in Chicago. One day, while visiting family in Mississippi, he tells his friends his girlfriend is white. They don't believe him—and dare him to ask a white woman at a store—Carolyn Bryant—out on a date.

What happens next goes on to be pretty widely disputed for years (though the truth comes out later on). Emmett enters the store. No one else is in there other than Carolyn. (That's important.) He leaves . . . and is heard saying "Bye, baby."

Carolyn claims Emmett grabbed her. Made vulgar advances. Wolf-whistled at her. Her husband—Roy Bryant—is not happy about this. A few days later, Roy and his half brother J. W. Milam show up at the house of Emmett's great-uncle.

They force Emmett into their car. Three days later, Emmett's corpse shows up in the Tallahatchie River, so disfigured and mutilated that the body is only identifiable by an initialed ring.

A lot happens all at once. Emmett's mom requests the body be sent to Chicago rather than immediately buried, like authorities want. She holds an open-casket funeral so the world can see what happened to her son. A popular Black magazine—*Jet*—publishes a picture of the corpse.

It goes the 1955 equivalent of viral.

Not two weeks later, Roy Bryant and J. W. Milam go on trial in a segregated courthouse. The jury is all white.

You probably won't be surprised to hear the outcome.

Not guilty on the murder charge. And not even indicted on the kidnapping charge.

Decades later, in 2017, it comes out that Carolyn Bryant made it all up.

I'll repeat: Carolyn made it all up.

Emmett never so much as touched her, let alone threatened or harassed her.

Just take a second to let that sink in.

People were outraged back then, too. And that outrage only grew a couple months after the acquittal, when a Black woman named Rosa Parks was jailed for refusing to give up her seat on a public bus in Montgomery, Alabama, to a white man—a direct violation of the city's racial segregation laws.

Here's where people first start hearing Martin Luther King Jr.'s name on a national level.

In response to Rosa Parks's imprisonment, King organizes the Montgomery Bus Boycott. You might know the story: the city's bus laws required Black people to sit at the back of the bus and give up seats to white riders if the front of the bus was full. Yes, really. So the Black community got together, said they'd had enough of that treatment, and refused to use the bus system until the laws were changed.

Fun fact: civil rights activists in Montgomery had been hoping to organize some kind of protest of this law for a while. Before Rosa Parks, there was Claudette Colvin, a Black fifteen-year-old who was arrested for refusing to move to the back of the bus and give up her seat to a white person. But some civil rights leaders didn't think Colvin would be a good icon for the movement, especially when compared to Parks, who was already the well-known and respected secretary of the Montgomery chapter of the NAACP.

So when Parks took action in 1955, civil rights activists were ready to join in. The Montgomery Bus Boycott ultimately led the US Supreme Court to shoot down Alabama state and Montgomery city bus segregation laws.

That's widely considered to be the start of the civil rights movement.

And the end of the United States as the world knew it.

1957

The movement only continues to pick up steam from there. A couple years later, sixty Black pastors and civil rights leaders from lots of southern states, including Martin Luther King Jr., get together in Atlanta, Georgia. The topic of discussion? Organizing nonviolent protests against racial discrimination and segregation.

The same year, nine Black students are blocked from going to Little Rock Central High School in Little Rock, Arkansas. Remember, racial segregation in public schools is illegal at this point—but that doesn't stop schools from trying to keep Black people out.

Eventually, Prez Dwight D. Eisenhower sends federal troops to escort the students—dubbed the Little Rock Nine—to school. And even then, they continue to be harassed.

Eisenhower makes another very important decision that year.

He signs the Civil Rights Act of 1957, which allows federal prosecution of anyone who tries to suppress the right to vote. This is a huge deal for lots of reasons, in particular because it's the first federal civil rights legislation passed since 1875 and because it starts taking steps toward making it easier for people of color to cast a ballot. Because, as with racial segregation in schools, while it was technically legal for people of color to vote . . . lots of states and counties did everything in their power to stop them from doing so.

1960

Ever seen those pictures of Black people sitting at "whites only" lunch counters in restaurants?

Here's where it started. Four Black college students in Greensboro, North Carolina, sit at one of those counters and absolutely refuse to leave without being served. Police show up . . . but aren't really able to do anything, since the college students (who go on to be known as the Greensboro Four) are nonviolent.

The Greensboro Four go the whole day without being served. The next day, even more Black students join them.

Just four days later, three hundred students gather at the restaurant. And soon, similar sit-ins are held throughout the country.

The sit-ins were significant for a lot of reasons. One: they brought a whole lot of media attention to the civil rights movement. And two: in the summer of 1960, more and more restaurants got less and less segregated.

Schools were starting to be less segregated, too. Case in point: Ruby Bridges. In 1960, the six-year-old became the first Black kid to attend the all-white William Frantz Elementary School in Louisiana. She wasn't welcomed.

Every day while walking into the school, Ruby—escorted by four federal marshals—was greeted by hordes of people screaming slurs. One white woman even held a Black baby doll in a coffin.

It didn't take long for every white student to ditch Ruby's class. And all but one teacher refused to teach her. Meanwhile, Ruby's dad lost his job, and grocery stores shook their heads to selling to her mom. Her grandparents, who worked and lived on a sharecropping farm, were kicked out.

The story gained national attention—and shows how even as the country was maybe moving forward legally, people still held on to its (even more) racist past.

1961

Say hello to the Freedom Riders, a group of white and Black civil rights activists (including John Lewis, who you might have heard of from his days in Congress) who took part in Freedom Rides—bus trips through the South to protest segregated buses and bus terminals.

This kind of thing wasn't new. In 1947, the Congress of Racial Equality—which also put together the Freedom Rides—organized the Journey of Reconciliation, which had white and Black activists taking bus rides to challenge segregation laws.

If you hadn't noticed yet, buses were definitely a big part of the civil rights movement.

So, let's get back to 1961. As the Freedom Riders made their

way through the South, they tried using whites-only restrooms, lunch counters, and waiting rooms.

Pretty peaceful, right?

The response . . . was decidedly not.

The Freedom Riders were brutally attacked. On one of their rides, angry mobs of hundreds of white people surrounded the bus. Then followed it in automobiles—forcing the bus to keep going to protect the passengers.

Eventually, the bus's tires blew out.

Someone threw a bomb into the bus.

The Freedom Riders fled. And were instantly beaten.

Freedom Riders on another bus faced a violent white mob, too. Some members of the mob held metal pipes. But when they arrived at the station in Birmingham, Alabama, no police were there to protect them—apparently because it was Mother's Day.

Yeah, right.

From there, the violence only got worse. After a short period of struggling to find a driver willing to take them, the Freedom Riders started up again—this time, under police escort. Buuuut it didn't take long for the police escort to totally abandon the Freedom Riders, leaving them to be beaten with baseball bats and clubs by yet another white mob.

(Was it still Mother's Day?)

Six hundred federal marshals were sent to stop the violence.

There were also times when some Freedom Riders were arrested for using whites-only facilities . . . and even sentenced to a month in jail.

All this time, the Freedom Rides gained national attention. Hundreds of people started taking part in the bus trips.

And months later . . . segregation in interstate transit terminals was banned.

At this point, I want to take a step back and note something really important. The violence and anger that we've been reading about, whether from these mobs attacking buses, or the Ruby Bridges harassers, or even the KKK—those sentiments weren't limited to just those very visible groups. Not even close. There were a fair number of people who were very much happy with the way things were (remember the rope?).

In fact, most white Americans weren't actually fans of Martin Luther King Jr. during the civil rights movement. They saw him as far too radical and felt far too uncomfortable with much of what he said and pushed for. The FBI even considered him one of the most dangerous men in the US.

King didn't just want to see the end of racism; he wanted to see the end of the system that allowed racism to thrive. He wanted a "reconstruction of society," a "revolution of values." He wanted the downfall of the rope.

It wasn't that there were specific US policies that he disliked. He didn't like US policy, period. He spoke of how the American gov had always been racist and pointed to white Americans' attempted annihilation of Native Americans as an example. He criticized America's version of capitalism and connected economic injustice and racial injustice. He talked about structural inequality. He was upset that he couldn't openly support ideas of democratic socialism.

If you didn't pick up on it yet, I'll make it clear: there are a ton of parallels here to our world right now, especially as it pertains to the racial justice movement. A lot of people are talking about the same things Martin Luther King Jr. was talking about many decades ago. And a lot of people are still questioning whether these things are too radical.

Just some food for thought.

1963

The civil rights movement is taken to the next level.

Two hundred and fifty thousand people take part in the March on Washington for Jobs and Freedom. You probably know the one.

That's the one where Martin Luther King Jr. gave his "I Have a Dream" speech. And said that there would be "neither rest nor tranquility in America" until Black

people were granted equal rights. Plus specifically touched on topics like police brutality and voter suppression (hint: those are both still issues today).

People were hopeful.

And then, not even a month later, a bomb at 16th Street Baptist Church in Birmingham, Alabama, killed four young Black girls ahead of Sunday services.

Thousands of people showed up in protest and in mourning. Violence broke out. Two Black men were killed—one of whom was killed by police. Countless protesters were arrested. And eventually, the National Guard was called in. (Sound familiar?)

As public fury grew, so did calls to arrest those responsible for the bombing.

And guess what?

No one answered those calls.

That's made even worse by the fact that in 1965, the FBI had info on the identity of the bombers . . . and literally just did nothing.

Like . . . nothing.

It wasn't until 1977, when Alabama's attorney general reopened the investigation, that justice was at least partly served. Ku Klux Klan leader Robert E. Chambliss was brought to trial and convicted of murder. He died in prison in 1985.

Over the next couple decades, more Klan members were convicted. The final bomber was sent to prison in 2002.

I'll repeat: 2002. Almost forty years after the bombing.

Yeah.

1964

The Civil Rights Act of 1964 gets a big thumbs-up from Prez Lyndon B. Johnson.

This act kind of changed everything for not just people of color, but all marginalized communities living in the United States. Case in point: it basically ended (legal) segregation in public places—plus banned employment discrimination on the basis of race, religion, sex, or national origin. Meaning people could no longer be fired due to any of those factors.

So yeah. It was a pretty huge deal.

And it still is. In June 2020, the Supreme Court ruled that the Civil Rights Act aaaalso protects LGBTQ+ people from discrimination in the workplace—a very necessary distinction, especially since, up until that ruling, it was legal in, oh, more than half of US states to fire workers for being gay, bisexual, or transgender.

1965

Malcom X is assassinated.

You'll notice Malcom X doesn't really take up as much of the

conversation around the civil rights movement as he probably should. As a Black nationalist, he was big on the idea of achieving equality through "any means necessary." At one point, while he was a member of the Nation of Islam, he saw white people as the devil (a popular Black nationalist belief). He changed his last name to X to reject the name that had been given to his ancestors by those who enslaved them. The FBI was pretty much always keeping tabs on him—and the agency's leader even told the New York office to "do something about" him.

Years later, he ditched the Nation of Islam due to corruption problems there and founded the Organization of Afro-American Unity. Its number one enemy? Racism, which the org saw as the single biggest obstacle to justice.

His voice, his power, his influence continued to grow from there.

And then, in 1965 . . . he was assassinated by Black Muslim men.

But his voice, his power, his influence lived on, shaping the US in one of the most transformative times in its history.

Another thing that shaped the US during the civil rights movement: the Selma-to-Montgomery marches, which kicked off in 1965.

Before I get into this, try to pick out the two main issues at play here as you read. I'll give you a hint: voter suppression and police brutality.

Hmmm.

Reminder: even though Black people could technically vote, and even though voter suppression was technically illegal . . . it was still very widespread (and, reminder—it still is today). Hint: in Selma,

Alabama, only 2 percent of eligible Black voters were actually able to register in 1964.

And as you may know, if you can't vote, you don't get nearly as much of a say in the gov compared to those who can—which extends

to not having as much of a say in which kinds of laws are being passed. In this case, civil rights laws.

That wasn't the only reason for the first march from Selma to Montgomery. In February 1965, white segregationists attacked peaceful protesters in Alabama, with a state trooper ultimately shooting and killing Jimmie Lee Jackson, a young Black protester.

Civil rights activists—including Martin Luther King Jr.—were outraged. So in March 1965, six hundred people started to march from Selma to Montgomery, Alabama, to protest voter suppression and register Black voters in the South.

They were met with violence.

Alabama state troopers carrying whips, nightsticks, and tear gas confronted the protesters at the Edmund Pettus Bridge. They attacked them brutally, so much so that the protesters were forced to turn back.

The violence was televised. It was dubbed Bloody Sunday. And it sparked an even greater protest.

Suddenly, hundreds of ministers, priests, rabbis, and social activists were making their way to Selma to join the march. It wasn't long before there were two thousand of them.

So a few weeks later, they tried again.

Yet again, they were met with state troopers—but after King led a prayer, they let them continue. But due to all sorts of laws that were designed to crack down on protests, King turned the protesters around. (Heads up: he got a whole lot of criticism for that from other activists who saw it as backing down.)

The same day, segregationists attacked another protester—a white minister named James Reeb. They beat him to death.

The march set off again another day. State officials tried to block it. A US court said *no way* and ordered Alabama to let the march go on.

Less than a week later, the US prez—Lyndon B. Johnson—gave a big speech on TV. He gave his support to the Selma protesters and sent US Army troops and National Guard forces to protect them. Finally, over a month after setting off on the first march, the marchers reached Montgomery.

By this point, fifty thousand people were marching. Speeches were made. And so was change.

The march gained national attention for voting rights. And not too long after it came to an end, Prez Johnson signed off on the Voting Rights Act of 1965.

Big, big deal.

The act specifically guaranteed the right to vote to all Black people. It also banned certain obstacles that had been preventing Black people from doing just that. Think: using literacy tests as a requirement for voting. Plus it said the gov could keep an eye on voter registration in any areas where those kinds of tests had been used—and the US attorney general could go out and legally challenge the use of poll taxes for state and local elections.

I'll repeat my "big, big deal."

(It's maybe important to note that these kinds of things aren't a one-and-done. In 2013, the gov made a loooot a lot of changes to this act, lessening the power of the federal gov to check up on states and make sure they're not suppressing votes, and ever since, there've been attempts to try to restore it. In case I haven't made it clear already, these are ongoing fights that we can impact by raising our voices today.)

1968

Martin Luther King Is Slain in Memphis; A White Is Suspected; Johnson Urges Calm (*The New York Times*)

You've heard the story. We all have.

King is standing on the second-floor balcony of his Memphis, Tennessee, hotel when a sniper's bullet hits him. He is rushed to a hospital . . . and proclaimed dead just an hour later. He is thirty-nine.

The country's reaction to King's death is intense. Lots of civil rights activists feel like his killing symbolizes the fact that much of white America is still not willing to grant Black people equal rights. Intro a mass radicalization that saw many moderate Black activists turning to the Black Power movement and the Black Panther

Party, whose purpose was, in part, to challenge police brutality via "copwatching"—open-carry armed citizens patrols.

There were some big legislative impacts, too. Cough, the Civil Rights Act of 1968, cough. Hugely significant, since it basically said everyone should get equal access to housing regardless of things like race, religion, or national origin. (Quick backstory: many Black Americans had—and unfortunately still do have—problems finding people who would rent or sell to them, particularly in majority-white neighborhoods.)

That was the effective end of the civil rights movement. I'll clue you in on why.

The movement sought to end racial discrimination and gain equal rights under the law.

And with the Civil Rights Act of 1968 (plus the Voting Rights Act of 1965, the Civil Rights Act of 1964, and the Civil Rights Act of 1957), civil rights activists achieved those goals. Well. Legally, at least.

Not only that, but they achieved those things for most Americans. Because of the civil rights movement, the US gov now had laws protecting every American, regardless of ethnicity, sex, or national origin.

Of course, this wasn't the end of racial injustice. If anything, learning about the civil rights movement makes it even clearer how far we have to go today. So much of what civil rights activists were fighting for in the 1950s and 1960s is stuff we're still fighting for at this very moment. Maybe those things look a little bit different, but that doesn't mean they're not still there and locking Black people out of rights and opportunities that have always been granted to white people.

To be super direct: that should be your takeaway from the civil rights movement. Not the rosy outlook of yeah, we had segregation, and that was racist, but then we solved it! No. We should look at the civil rights movement and marvel at the power we have when we all stand up against racism. We should marvel at just how much change we're able to make.

And then we should take a very serious look at our society today and recognize all the change that still needs to be made—and know that those changes are possible, if only we keep up the fight.

The LGBTQ+ Rights Movement

ICYMI, the (legal) fight for LGBTQ+ rights is one that's very, very current (meanwhile, the fight for societal acceptance has been going on for ages). LGBTQ+ people are still legally persecuted in many countries around the world today—and even in the US, it wasn't until 2015 that same-sex marriage was finally legalized at the national level.

Think about that. 2015.

You read all about homophobia, biphobia, and transphobia earlier in this book. But it can be hard to grasp just how prominent and admissible all those things were in the United States back in the early 1900s.

The Studies, the Reports, and the Laws

Until as recently as several decades ago, homophobia was basically considered to be backed by science. No, really. There were all kinds of studies and reports detailing aaaall the ways in which LGBTQ+ people were allegedly inferior—and not only that, but straight-up dangerous.

See: a 1950 Senate report called "Employment of Homosexuals and Other Sex Perverts in Government." You read that right.

For years, the US gov had been secretly investigating employees' sexual orientation. Anyone discovered to be gay or lesbian was discharged from the military or fired from the gov in what became known as the "Lavender Scare." Thousands of people lost their jobs.

At the end of the gov's investigation, they deposited the aforementioned report on the desk of every member of Congress. Its findings?

Homosexuality is a mental illness.

Homosexuals "constitute security risks" to the nation.

Homosexuals engage in "overt acts of perversion." And thus "lack the emotional stability of normal persons."

Two years later, the American Psychiatric Association listed homosexuality as a "sociopathic personality disturbance." But the label did get some backlash, since it wasn't exactly backed up by scientific data. (Big shocker.)

A year after that? Prez Eisenhower signed Executive Order 10540, which banned gay people from working for the federal gov or any of its private contractors. The why: they were apparently determined to be risks, along with alcoholics and "neurotics." (Important thing to keep in mind: Eisenhower's been applauded for all the strides he made during the civil rights movement. But even as the nation was definitely progressing in some ways, it was staying pretty darn stagnant in others.)

But then came a report that changed everything, mostly because it was one of the first reports on LGBTQ+ people that wasn't totally against LGBTQ+ people. A woman named Evelyn Hooker shared research revealing that heterosexual men and homosexual men don't differ significantly in any biological or psychological way. And, while it sounds kind of obvious, this was actually a big, big deal at the time. You could say it revolutionized the way the medical community thought of gay people. In particular: it scientifically destroyed the belief that being gay was a mental illness.

For perhaps the first time, public perception began to shift, too . . .

The Organizations

Over the years, there have been a number of different organizations working to fight for LGBTQ+ rights. They didn't always last very long, because of things like political pressure, police raids, or just not enough public support. Think: organizations like the Society for Human Rights, which was the first recognized gay rights organization in the US, but which was disbanded after several of its members were arrested within the span of a few months. Then there was the Daughters of Bilitis, which was the first lesbian civil and political rights group in the US. There was also the Mattachine Society, which worked to protect and improve the rights of gay men (but you'll hear more about them in a bit).

But slowly, the movement began to get off the ground. And slowly, change started taking place.

1958. The Supreme Court made its very first ruling in favor of LGBTQ+ people. It said the LGBTQ+ magazine *One: The Homosexual Viewpoint* had the same First Amendment rights as any other magazine.

Four years later, Illinois became the first US state to decriminalize homosexuality.

Oh, did I mention? Not only was same-sex marriage illegal—it was actually illegal to be gay at the time.

So yeah. LGBTQ+ rights activists were up against a whole lot.

Luckily, they were willing to fight.

The Protests
1959

Police officers enter Cooper Do-nuts, a popular café in downtown Los Angeles, and begin harassing patrons. Eventually, they try to arrest two drag queens, two male sex workers, and a gay man. That leads onlookers to begin throwing coffee, donuts, cups, trash—basically whatever they could find—at the police until they drive away without making any arrests. But riots continue until more police show up, block the street, and detain several people.

It's believed to be the first gay uprising in the US.

1965

Picketers stage the first Reminder Day to call attention to the lack of basically any civil rights whatsoever for LGBTQ+ people. The protests continue every year for the next four years.

1966

Members of the Mattachine Society, a prominent LGBTQ+ rights organization, stage a "sip-in" at the Julius' bar in New York's Greenwich Village. For context: the New York Liquor Authority didn't let bars serve gay patrons—apparently because they were "disorderly." (Major eye roll.)

The Mattachine Society is immediately denied service . . . so they sue. In response, the New York City Commission on Human Rights says *We hear you loud and clear* and declares gay people have the right to be served.

Same year. Management calls the police on a group of trans women inside Gene Compton's Cafeteria in San Francisco. A police officer gets rough with a patron, who apparently throws coffee in his face.

It sparks a riot.

People rush out into the street and destroy police and public property. Later, activists put together the National Transsexual Counseling Unit. It's the first peer-run support and advocacy organization in the world. Literally.

Back it up: it wasn't unusual for transgender people to face police abuse. What was unusual? Actually standing up to the police.

So you can imagine just how significant of a moment this was.

But what was arguably the most significant moment of the LGBTQ+ rights movement didn't come until three years later.

1969

Reminder: LGBTQ+ people could now be served alcohol. Only a slight problem . . . it was still illegal to engage in any sort of "gay behavior" in public. Think: holding hands, kissing, or dancing with someone of the same perceived sex . . . you get the gist. So there were a fair number of gay bars and clubs throughout New York where LGBTQ+ people could feel somewhat safe.

Emphasis on somewhat. Police raids on gay bars and clubs were pretty common. But on June 28, 1969, people at the Stonewall Inn in Greenwich Village grew tired of the constant harassment.

I'll fill you in.

Police entered the club. Arrested thirteen people. Manhandled even more. Took people suspected of violating the state's "gender-appropriate clothing statute," which basically said you needed to dress in clothes that lined up with your sex assigned at birth, into the bathroom to forcibly examine their genitals. Hit a lesbian woman over the head while forcing her into a police van.

She shouted:

"Take action."

That single shout changed everything.

The growing crowd listened. And threw pennies, bottles, cobblestones, and basically whatever they could at the police.

It didn't take long for it to blow up into a riot involving hundreds of people. The police—plus some prisoners and a writer—barricaded themselves inside the Stonewall Inn. The crowd followed them . . . and even tried to set fire to the bar.

The fire dept and a riot squad soon showed up, put out the flames, and rescued those inside. But the protests didn't end there. Over the next five days, thousands of people kept demonstrating around the Stonewall Inn.

The impact was immeasurable.

Think of the fire at Stonewall as lighting a fire all across the United States. The protests left LGBTQ+ rights activists feeling more empowered than ever before.

Don't believe me?

The following year saw the first gay pride parade. Three years after that, the American Psychiatric Association board removed homosexuality from its list of mental illness. In the following years, Kathy Kozachenko and Harvey Milk became the first openly gay elected officials in the history of the US.

But it was still an uphill battle.

1977

Eight years after the Stonewall Inn riots. Dade County in Florida passed a gay rights ordinance—making Florida the fortieth US state to do so. But singer and ex–beauty queen Anita Bryant wasn't a fan of the news—and immediately set about getting the ordinance repealed.

She succeeded in just six weeks.

Not a typo.

I'll repeat: Stonewall emboldened LGBTQ+ activists across the US, who made great progress. But on the flip side, Anita Bryant's efforts to ax that gay rights ordinance led other cities and states nation-wide to do the same. In fact, it was so impactful that Bryant actually started an organization dedicated to keeping gay people oppressed: Save Our Children Inc.

"Homosexuals cannot reproduce, so they must recruit."

That's a direct quote from Bryant's organization—and it became a driving factor for lots of anti-gay-rights activists throughout the

US. It's all based on those enduring stereotypes I outlined in the Homophobia, Biphobia, and Transphobia chapter earlier in the book—that gay people are, well, perverts.

Remember **Harvey Milk**? It was right around this time that he started to become especially significant in the fight for LGBTQ+ rights. As gay rights ordinances were being trashed across the US, Milk intro'd a new ordinance in San Francisco that protected gay and lesbian people from being fired from their jobs due to their sexualities. Plus led a (successful) campaign against a policy that would have forbid the hiring of LGBTQ+ teachers.

The same month, he was assassinated. By San Francisco ex–city supervisor Dan White.

White's motives were ultimately found to be jealousy and depression—not homophobia. But what really got people angry was that six months later, he was convicted of voluntary manslaughter and sentenced to a grand total of seven years in prison.

So yeah. Cue major protests.

See: five thousand people ransacked San Francisco City Hall. The following night, ten thousand people gathered to commemorate what would have been Milk's forty-ninth birthday.

Now let's fast-forward to 1993. (And yes, if you noticed we skipped over ACT UP and AIDS—that's because we get into that a little later in this book. See: Diseases.) Things start to get a bit murky. The US Dept of Defense announces a new directive that basically says the US military can't bar applicants from service based on sexual orientation. In theory, that sounds great . . . but it birthed "Don't Ask, Don't Tell." Aka the idea that military applicants couldn't be asked about their sexual orientation. It kinda sorta also stipulated that LGBTQ+

people serving in the military couldn't talk about their sexual orientation or engage in any sort of sexual activity. So naturally, it got a lot of criticism from gay rights activists for pretty much forcing LGBTQ+ people into secrecy.

Three years later, things got a lot clearer—and a lot worse. Prez Bill Clinton signed off on the Defense of Marriage Act, which defined marriage as a legal union between—wait for it—one man and one woman.

But despite all these setbacks, things ultimately continued to progress.

Okay. So let's bring things up to the year 2000. Let's take a quick pause to acknowledge how many years have gone by since the start of this chapter. (Cough, seventy-six, cough.) Let's also take a quick pause to acknowledge that same-sex marriage STILL has not been fully legalized in the US at this point—or even in a single US state. Yes way. (Some states have made marriage rulings in favor of same-sex couples, but it still isn't even close to the kind of legal rights activists are seeking.)

The 2000s were a big decade for LGBTQ+ rights. A lot started happening all at once. But it's important to keep in mind that it was still all happening pretty late, considering how long the fight for LGBTQ+ rights has been around.

Vermont Gives Final Approval to Same-Sex Unions
(*The New York Times*, 2000)

The Supreme Court: Homosexual Rights; Justices, 6–3, Legalize Gay Sexual Conduct in Sweeping Reversal of Court's '86 Ruling (*The New York Times*, 2003)

Gay Rights Leap Forward as Massachusetts Becomes the State of Wedded Bliss (*The Guardian*, 2004)

Dems Face Sharp Questions on Gay Rights (CBS News, 2007)

Obama OKs Some Benefits for Employees' Same-Sex Partners (CNN, 2009)

Senate Votes to Repeal 'Don't Ask, Don't Tell' (NPR, 2010)

New York Allows Same-Sex Marriage, Becoming Largest State to Pass Law (*The New York Times*, 2011)

Obama Administration Drops Legal Defense of "Marriage Act" (ABC News, 2011)

2015

Drumroll, please. The Supreme Court declares same-sex marriage legal in all fifty states.

2015 is also the cutoff year for Generation Z (as in, it's the last year anyone counted in our generation was born). You read that right. Most of the United States' strides in LGBTQ+ rights . . . came while most Gen Zers were still kids. So while our generation often takes LGBTQ+ rights for granted, it's vital that we all remember that it wasn't that long ago that LGBTQ+ people had far fewer rights than they even do now.

And, ICYMI, the Supreme Court is still making very important rulings on LGBTQ+ rights. See: that June 2020 Supreme Court decision I mentioned back in the Civil Rights Movement chapter, which said the Civil Rights Act aaaalso protects LGBTQ+ people from discrimination in the workplace.

Because, PSA: LGBTQ+ people still face oppression and injustice in the US (and around the world). Even legally. The US is a place that lets a baker refuse to bake a cake for a gay couple due to religious reasons. The US is a place that has eleven states handing taxpayer money to adoption agencies that deny services to LGBTQ+ people.

Need I go on?

So, how about a pact:

Let's make sure LGBTQ+ people aren't forced to keep fighting for rights when the next generation is born.

Let's make sure the need for an LGBTQ+ rights movement ends with Gen Z. (Because, yes—it's still very needed, all these years later.)

Let's be the ones to put an end to this fight, once and for all.

The Arab Spring

Join me in the year 2010. Our story here starts with Tunisia, a country in North Africa considered to be part of the Middle East. It's important to point out that Tunisia's gov, while super corrupt, was actually on pretty solid ground. There was no slow descent, no signs of splintering. Absolutely no one predicted what was about to happen—and absolutely no one thought it would be successful.

Meet Mohamed Bouazizi, a twenty-six-year-old who sold fruit from a cart in the Tunisian town of Sidi Bouzid. Again, Tunisia had lots of problems surrounding gov corruption—and Bouazizi was just one of the many Tunisians who were greatly affected by these problems. See: local officials would repeatedly demand bribes and steal his merchandise.

So Bouazizi set himself on fire.

This single act went on to symbolize the anger many Tunisians were feeling over a long list of injustices and hardships (including high unemployment, poverty, and a harsh gov).

You may have noticed that most of these movements have the Moment: the Moment that changes everything. I like to think of it as a breaking point. The rising tensions of the Vietnam War brought the hippie movement to a new level, and the tragic murder of Emmett Till and Rosa Parks's brave stand did similar things for the civil rights movement. Bouazizi's act of protest was Tunisia's Moment, Tunisia's breaking point—and it led to massive demonstrations throughout the country that saw dozens of protesters killed in violent clashes with police. Not long after, Tunisia's prez, Zine al-Abidine Ben Ali, took to everyone's TV screens to pinkie promise not to seek re-election when his term ended in 2014. Plus pledged to cut food prices and gov restrictions on internet use.

But protesters still weren't satisfied—and kept taking to the streets. The death toll kept rising, too.

The following day, Tunisia declared a state of emergency. Dissolved its gov. And set a date for new legislative elections.

But the protests raged on.

So Ben Ali stepped down as prez.

The protests didn't slow for another few days, until the country's acting prime minister announced the formation of a new unity gov that included lots of opposition figures. This new gov intro'd a set of reforms that did things like lift Ben Ali's ban on opposition political parties and grant amnesty to all political prisoners.

In just a month, Tunisia's gov had been almost totally transformed in what became known as the Jasmine Revolution. (That transformation was truly complete in December 2011, after Tunisians participated in their first free election and drafted a new constitution, and a democratically chosen prez and prime minister took office.)

Intro another Moment.

Countries throughout the rest of the Middle East had been paying close attention to the Tunisian revolt. Specifically, Egypt—where there was already lots of unrest.

I'll fill you in.

In June 2010, Khaled Said, a young computer science programmer and bizman, died while in police custody in the Egyptian city of Alexandria. Cue major accusations of police brutality—especially when a photo of Said's battered face was posted online.

Wael Ghonim, a twenty-nine-year-old Google marketing exec, saw the picture and immediately set up a Facebook page. Its name? "We Are All Khaled Said."

"Today they killed Khaled. If I don't act for his sake, tomorrow they will kill me."

That's a direct quote from Ghonim's Facebook page—and it resonated. Big time.

Over the next few months, hundreds of thousands of people followed the page. Calls for Egypt's gov to resign began brewing.

That brings us to January 2011.

Enter: Hassan Mostafa, an Egyptian activist.

Mostafa sent a quick text to his friends. He got to the point:

Ben Ali gone. Possibility.

Mostafa wasn't the only one who felt this way. For the first time, Egyptians saw a real opportunity to rise up against their leaders—all because of Tunisia. And it was an opportunity people didn't pass up.

The People of Egypt
1 hour ago

Intro: the Day of Revolution on January 25, a massive wave of protests that were largely organized via Facebook and Twitter—which got the word out to more people than ever before and also served to help spread fake info to divert police away from demonstrators.

It quickly became clear Egypt was going through a full-on revolution, Tunisia style.

But the gov was determined to hold on to its power.

By any means necessary.

Hundreds were injured and even killed as Egypt's military and security forces clashed with protesters. The gov also tried to give in to protesters just the teeniest bit in an attempt to cool things down—but as in Tunisia, it didn't work.

What did work? Three more weeks of protests. And the military declaring it wouldn't keep using force against protesters.

That was it. Egypt's prez, Hosni Mubarak, knew he and his gov had lost.

On February 11, Mubarak was removed from office by the military after nearly thirty years.

But it wasn't all happy endings. The new gov was run by the military—and it wasn't super eager to begin a full transition of power to a democratically elected gov. And when people protested, the military and security forces . . . got violent again.

This kind of violence went on for months and didn't really end until parliamentary elections eventually took place in late November 2011. By January 2012, things were looking up again: the newly elected People's Assembly held its inaugural session.

So that's two for two.

Two countries.

Two revolutions.

Two new governments.

All of a sudden, everyone wanted to get in on this wave of change.

Yemen

The first prodemocracy protests popped up here not long after Ben Ali was kicked out in Tunisia. The central state (aka the gov) was already super weak, so when these protests broke out, it quickly splintered. Lots of tribal and military leaders sided with the pro-testers, which was a really big deal since these kinds of groups

usually didn't mix . . . but negotiations to remove the Yemeni prez from power didn't exactly go as planned. See: loyalist and opposition fighters clashed. And the violence didn't end there. It got so bad that the international community had to get involved—which ultimately led the Yemeni prez to sign off on an agreement that basically said he'd give up his job to the vice prez. Even then, the war continued to rage—and, in fact, still does to this day.

Bahrain

This was a country that was steeped in political and economic problems. And in mid-February 2011, massive protests over these problems broke out—largely led by human rights activists and members of Bahrain's marginalized Shiite Muslim community. The gov responded in turn. Extremely violently. Things were made worse by the fact that Saudi Arabia and the United Arab Emirates sent over soldiers to help out Bahrain's gov. As a result . . . the protests were stifled within weeks. Dozens of alleged protest leaders were convicted of antigov activity . . . and jailed. Hundreds of people (mostly Shiite) suspected of supporting the protests were fired. And dozens of Shiite mosques were destroyed by the gov.

Libya

These protests started up in mid-February 2011, too. And they eventually turned just as violent. As in the gov immediately responded with full military force. In response, protesters took up a fully armed revolt against the Libyan regime of Muammar al-Qaddafi. The international community got involved yet again, with NATO launching air strikes targeting Qaddafi's forces. Just months later, Qaddafi was forced from power and killed. But the new gov—known as the Transitional National Council (aka TNC)—faced lots of problems as it worked to restart the economy, establish a working gov, and keep all the tribal militias that had taken part in the rebellion in check in order to prevent another outbreak of violence. A big part of that was because outside powers like Qatar, the United Arab Emirates, and Egypt kept meddling with things.

Syria

These protests broke out about a month after the ones in Libya and Bahrain—and had protesters calling for Prez Bashar al-Assad to quit. The gov responded with a brutal crackdown. And that kind of became the theme in Syria, with the following years seeing an uptick in violence and increasing condemnation from the international community and human rights groups. Ultimately, Assad clung to power. He continues to fight to keep hold of that power as of this writing, in one of the world's most disastrous civil wars.

There were also changes throughout the rest of the Middle East—not full-on revolutions, but concessions from govs that definitely wanted to avoid any sort of unrest.

All of the above became known as the Arab Spring revolutions. And they were massively significant in more ways than one.

They led to a series of massive protests. They toppled govs previously thought to be un-topple-able. They caused a pattern of violence and unrest and infighting in many countries—a pattern that still stands today. They shaped the dynamic of the Middle East as the world knew it. They caused an immigration crisis the likes of which had never been seen before, a crisis that also incited racism, xenophobia, and Islamophobia throughout Europe, where many migrants fled. Lots of problems were solved; lots weren't.

But like I said—they were significant in one other way, too. And this way was felt around the world.

Because of the Arab Spring, social media was cemented as a powerful tool for change-making—and its influence was only continuing to grow . . .

Black Lives Matter

You might know Black Lives Matter as the movement against police brutality. Or maybe you know it as the aftermath of anger and frustration over the killings of people such as Trayvon Martin and Michael Brown . . . and more recently, George Floyd and Breonna Taylor. Maybe you even know it for aaaaall the controversy (ever heard of #BlueLivesMatter or #AllLivesMatter?).

Point being: Black Lives Matter changed the game when it comes to social and political movements. Like, forever.

We'll start at the very, very beginning. Picture this: it's about seven p.m. in a rich neighborhood in Sanford, Florida. Think: it's gated, there's a clubhouse and a pool . . . you get the idea. There's this guy patrolling the neighborhood in a car, and he sees a teenager walking down the street. The guy suddenly grabs his phone.

SHORTENED TRANSCRIPT OF PHONE CALL WITH SANFORD POLICE DEPT

"Hey, we've had some break-ins in my neighborhood, and there's a real suspicious guy . . .

This guy looks like he's up to no good, or he's on drugs or something. It's raining and he's just walking around, looking about."

"Okay, and this guy is he white, Black, or Hispanic?"

"He looks Black."

"Did you see what he was wearing?"

"Yeah. A dark hoodie, like a gray hoodie, and either jeans or sweatpants and white tennis shoes . . .

He was just staring . . ."

"Okay, he's just walking around the area . . ."

". . . looking at all the houses."

"Okay . . ."

"Now he's just staring at me . . . Yeah, now he's coming towards me."

"Okay."

"He's got his hand in his waistband. And he's a Black male."

"How old would you say he looks?"

". . . late teens."

"Late teens, okay."

"Something's wrong with him. Yup, he's coming to check me out, he's got something in his hands, I don't know what his deal is."

"Just tell me if he does anything, okay—"

"How long until you get an officer over here?"

"Yeah, we've got someone on the way, just let me know if this guy does anything else."

"Okay. These assholes they always get away . . . Shit, he's running."

"He's running? Which way is he running?"

"Down towards the other entrance to the neighborhood."

"Which entrance is that that he's heading towards?"

"The back entrance . . . fucking [unintelligible]"

"Are you following him?"

"Yeah"

"Okay, we don't need you to do that."

"Okay."

"All right, sir, what is your name?"

"George . . . He ran."

"All right, George, what's your last name?"

"Zimmerman."

It's still not all that clear what happened next. What is clear: soon after, a neighbor called 911.

TRANSCRIPT OF FIRST NEIGHBOR'S 911 PHONE CALL

"911. Do you need police, fire, or medical?"

"Um, maybe both. I'm not sure, there's just someone screaming outside."

"Okay, and is it a male or a female?"

"It sounds like a male."

"And you don't know why?"

"I don't know why, I think they're yelling help, but I don't know. Just send someone quick please."

"Does he look hurt to you?"

"I can't see him, I don't want to go out there, I don't know what's going on so . . ."

From there, the 911 calls just kept coming.

"Someone's yelling . . . screaming, hollering 'help, help, help.'"

"Someone's screaming 'help' and I . . . heard a bang."

"I just heard a shot right behind my house."

"I think someone's been shot."

You just heard the end of Trayvon Martin's life. He's the unarmed seventeen-year-old Black youth who George Zimmerman called the Sanford Police Dept about.

You also heard the start of one of the greatest movements of our time.

What Zimmerman didn't know was that Martin's dad lived in the neighborhood. He didn't know that Martin was heading back home from a 7-Eleven, where he'd just bought Skittles and Arizona iced tea.

What Martin didn't know was that Zimmerman was the neighborhood watch guy. He didn't know that Zimmerman had a gun.

What neither of them knew was that the story would make headlines.

Family of Florida Boy Killed by Neighborhood Watch Seeks Arrest (Reuters)

Florida Family Seeks Justice after Unarmed Teen Shot by Neighborhood Watch Captain (ABC News)

"He Had a Gun, and Trayvon Had Skittles": Family Demands Justice as "Neighbourhood Watch Captain Who Shot Dead Unarmed Teen" Still Hasn't Been Charged

(*Daily Mail*)

Florida Teen's Shooting by Watchman Questioned (CNN)

US Opens Inquiry in Killing of Trayvon Martin

(*The New York Times*)

Was Trayvon Martin's Killing a Federal Hate Crime? (NPR)

Rallies and Protests Are Breaking Out Everywhere over the Trayvon Martin Shooting (Business Insider)

Just weeks after Martin's death gained national attention, the Dept of Justice announced it had opened up an investigation into the shooting.

That's when everything changed.

Up until then, Prez Barack Obama had kept his lips sealed on Martin's killing. Not anymore. In a speech, Obama said that if he "had a son, he'd look like Trayvon." Plus said that thinking about Martin made him think about his own kids. The prez said the country needed to investigate "every aspect" of the "tragedy" and do some "soul searching to figure out how does something like this happen."

The reaction was mixed. Some—like activists—applauded his comments. Others . . . not so much. See: they pointed fingers at Prez Obama for targeting Zimmerman.

Suddenly, more and more people began taking Zimmerman's side.

New pictures of George Zimmerman and Trayvon Martin appeared online. Zimmerman's picture was clear. He was wearing a suit and tie and grinning.

Martin's picture . . . was not actually Martin. We'll repeat: people were spreading around a blurry picture of a Black shirtless youth wearing a knit cap and giving the camera the middle finger . . . and acting like it was Trayvon Martin.

That viral photo was only a small, small part of the effort to twist Martin's image. The headlines began shifting—and so did the case.

Trayvon Martin Shooter Told Cops Teenager Went for His Gun (ABC News)

Trayvon Martin Case: He Was Suspended Three Times and Caught with "Burglary Tool" (Daily Mail)

Trayvon Martin's Tweets Show a Violent Trayvon, Critics Say (Digital Journal)

Trayvon Martin Had Traces of Marijuana in His System (Reuters)

Everyone from John Legend and Janelle Monáe to Donald Trump and Bill O'Reilly weighed in. Thousands of people participated in protests calling for Zimmerman's arrest. See: the "Million Hoodie March"—named after the black hoodie Martin was wearing when he was shot. Millions signed a petition. Others saw Zimmerman as a victim.

Fast-forward to April 11, 2012, and George Zimmerman was charged with second-degree murder and manslaughter. You read that right. The gov said Zimmerman profiled and confronted Martin—then shot him to death—all while Martin was committing no crimes.

As the months went on, the case continued to gain national attention. It ignited a widespread debate over racial profiling and civil rights—a debate that only intensified as Zimmerman headed to court.

Enter: July 13, 2013—well over a year after Zimmerman shot and killed Martin. A verdict was reached.

The six-woman jury sided with Zimmerman, who said the whole thing was done in self-defense after Martin allegedly knocked him to the ground, punched him, and slammed his head repeatedly against the sidewalk. (Meanwhile, the prosecution argued that Zimmerman purposely went after Martin and started a fight with him because he assumed he was a criminal.)

The acquittal was met with controversy. A whole lot of it. The protests escalated. The NAACP's prez, Benjamin Todd Jealous, said the organization was "outraged and heartbroken" over the verdict. Then promised to "pursue civil rights charges" with the Justice Dept—plus work to get "racial profiling in all its forms" outlawed.

He wasn't the only one who was upset.

Meet Alicia Garza, Patrisse Cullors, and Opal Tometi.

On July 13, 2013, they didn't know they were about to create one of the defining movements of our time. They didn't even really know each other.

It all started with a Facebook post from Alicia Garza.

black people. I love you. I love us. Our lives matter.

Patrisse Cullors agreed. And hit Post on this message.

declaration: black bodies will no longer be sacrificed for the rest of the world's enlightenment. i am done. i am so done. trayvon, you are loved infinitely #blacklivesmatter

The hashtag—inspired by Garza's post—connected. It popped up in a growing number of social media posts and even made appear-

ances at protests.

Suddenly, the movement had a name.

The hashtag caught fire. It got right to the heart of people's anger over Trayvon

Martin's death . . . and George Zimmerman's acquittal. In short: #BlackLivesMatter became the catalyst for change—serving as a singular message uniting the protests.

#BlackLivesMatter was no longer just about Martin. It described the frustration and anger Black people felt in a still racist and discriminatory US, decades after the civil rights movement and over 150 years after slavery was abolished.

Opal Tometi recognized the power of #BlackLivesMatter. She slid into Garza's DMs and volunteered to build a digital platform for the movement. Her dream: to build a community of activists and protesters who'd raise their voices for Black rights.

Enter: August 2014, just over a year after Zimmerman's acquittal. Michael Brown, an eighteen-year-old Black youth, was killed by a white police officer in Ferguson, Missouri. The US had déjà vu.

The protests were instant. You can thank the Black Lives Matter movement for that.

The organization created a "freedom ride" to bring protesters across the country to Ferguson. Hundreds of people took part, gaining the killing national attention. And the protests weren't limited to just Ferguson—there were also protests all across the US.

And as the months and years went on, Black Lives Matter helped spur protests over a growing number of killings.

Trayvon Martin's death was only the beginning.

love, K
@Heyy_MissCarter

I can't believe this is the world we live in. Everyday my heart breaks a little more. 💔😔 #BlackLivesMatter

1:55 PM · Aug 14, 2014 · Twitter for iPhone

---

psykadelikmofo
@Griggsy_Griggs

Im legitimately afraid of being gunned downed walking down the street, just for being in my skin #BlackLivesMatter

4:08 PM · Aug 14, 2014 · Twitter for iPhone

---

grannystanding4Truth
@granny_st

Why does the color of a murdered victim's skin, in America land of the free, automatically, condemn them for their death? #BlackLivesMatter

6:41 PM · Aug 31, 2014 · Twitter Web Client

Uneak Tershai
@UneakTershai

Truth is we are all one bullet away from being a hashtag #BlackLivesMatter #PleaseDontShoot #RallyForJustice #FightForPeace

6:47 PM · Aug 19, 2014 · Twitter for iPhone

Preston Mitchum, he/him ✔
@PrestonMitchum

Our Black skin is the problem. Our skin is the target. We could be doing NOTHING, yet they will say we do everything. #BlackLivesMatter

1:46 PM · Aug 10, 2014 · Twitter for iPhone

SpeakOut Speakers
@SpeakOutIDEC

Yesterday students across the nation honored Michael Brown by walking out. Civil Rights movement 2.0 #Ferguson #BlackLivesMatter

11:39 AM · Aug 26, 2014 · Twitter for iPad

"I Can't Breathe": Eric Garner Put in Chokehold
by NYPD Officer (*The Guardian*)

Death of Victorville Man Tasered Multiple Times
by Deputy Ruled Accidental (*Los Angeles Times*)

Tony Robinson Shooting: No Charges for Wisconsin
Police Officer (NBC News)

No Charges against LAPD Officers Who Shot and Killed
Ezell Ford, D.A. Says (*Los Angeles Times*)

Grand Jury Clears Cleveland Cops in Tanisha Anderson's
Death (Cleveland.com)

Cleveland Policeman Who Shot Tamir Rice Is Fired, but
Not Because of the 12-Year-Old's Death (*Los Angeles Times*)

Minnesota Officer Acquitted in Killing of Philando Castile
(*The New York Times*)

John Crawford III Case: Feds Announce No Charges for
Officer in Fatal 2014 Shooting (NBC News)

Prosecutors Won't Seek Third Trial for Former Ohio
Police Officer Who Shot Samuel DuBose
(*The Washington Post*)

Federal Officials Decline Prosecution in the Death
of Freddie Gray (US Department of Justice)

No Charges against Officers in Alton Sterling Death (CNN)

Tulsa Police Officer Who Killed Unarmed Black Man
Won't Face Civil Rights Charges (*The New York Times*)

The above headlines were only a small, small part of the thousands of police killings that occurred in the years following Martin's death. And for each one, Black Lives Matter fought for justice. Even though they weren't always all that successful in court, their protests and campaigns created a rising movement that brought awareness to modern-day civil rights issues.

And, BTW, this is another really good example of that whole rope analogy I talked about at the beginning of this section. Not only was progress hindered by those in power, but it was also hindered by those who were comfortable with the way things were and by those who didn't really think cutting the rope and forcefully challenging the systems that allowed these police killings to happen was that great of an idea.

But the movement grew anyway, and here's one of the biggest takeaways. Black Lives Matter is largely credited with creating the first-ever social media mobilization movement. We'll break it down. By creating a shareable message—cough, a hashtag, cough—Black Lives Matter was able to effectively go viral, spread its message, and get people all over the world to take part. Sound familiar? Hint: #MeToo, #TimesUp, #EnoughIsEnough, #NeverAgain, and #FridaysForFuture aaaaall follow a similar idea (and you'll read more about all of these in a minute). Think of #BlackLivesMatter as the start of intentional social media activism.

I'll elaborate. The pretty darn incredible thing about social media activism is that it gives every single human being the opportunity to have their voice and their stories heard. It lets anyone, wherever or whoever they are, take part in a rising movement—or maybe even create their own.

Now let's fast-forward to 2020, eight years after the killing of Trayvon Martin and seven years after the creation of Black Lives Matter.

A video comes out showing white police officer Derek Chauvin driving his knee into George Floyd's neck and kneeling on it for about nine minutes, killing him. A few months earlier, the US had become enraged after the police killing of Breonna Taylor, an innocent woman who police shot in her own home.

You probably know what happened next.

Massive protests—the biggest ever in the United States. Calls for accountability and change the likes of which our generation had never seen before. New education on systemic racism and privilege and all the things that make racism so deeply rooted and keep it so alive. Steps toward progress, not just within some police departments but also within industries like fashion and entertainment. The rise or reintroduction of social media movements—#DefundThePolice, #ACAB... you've heard them all. It was a moment when many people learned the term "antiracist" and tried to incorporate that idea into their lives and their actions.

Louisville-Taylor Family $12M Settlement Includes Police Reforms (*News and Tribune*)

Oscars: Future Films Must Meet Diversity and Inclusion Rules (NPR)

How Black Lives Matter Changed the Way Americans Fight for Freedom (ACLU)

Minneapolis Lawmakers Vow to Disband Police Department in Historic Move (*The Guardian*)

New York City Will Take $1 Billion from Police Budget (*USA Today*)

Half of the Nation's Largest Police Departments Have Banned or Limited Neck Restraints Since [George Floyd's Death] (*The Washington Post*)

The [Confederate] Statues Brought Down Since the George Floyd Protests Began (*The Atlantic*)

Grammy Awards to Rename Controversial 'Urban' Category (CNN)

Johnson & Johnson Will Stop Selling Skin-Whitening Lotions (*The New York Times*)

This second wave of the Black Lives Matter movement shifted things dramatically. It shifted the narrative and the discourse around race in the United States, and it brought about a renewed sense of urgency. Even more than that, it shifted the movement from social media and individual protests to everyday life for more people than ever before. Racism in the US could no longer be ignored.

It's perhaps both tragic and comforting to know that #BlackLivesMatter has lasted so long—and will likely continue to have this kind of power for years to come. Maybe you think that absolutely nothing has changed over the past decade. Maybe you think that everything has. But the real truth is somewhere in between: #BlackLivesMatter helped bring us to where we are today. It helped ignite a movement—and then reignite it several years later. But the work is far from over. Now it's in our hands to keep the fight going.

Me Too

In the last chapter, you saw how social media became a powerful organizing tool. You saw how social media gave a voice to a movement. But social media had yet to *be* the movement. You'll see what I mean in a second.

Our story starts in 2006. Tarana Burke coins the hashtag #MeToo to help women who have experienced sexual violence feel less alone.

Now let's fast-forward to a decade later. It's 2016, and an infamous *Access Hollywood* tape just came out. Millions of women hear Donald Trump brag about how being a celebrity lets you just *"grab [women] by the p*ssy."*

Not long after, he is elected prez.

And women all over the country decide they've had enough. They're used to men being able to get away with things like this, and they're angry. They want to speak out and take back some of the power.

Enter: the 2017 Women's March, one of the biggest protests in US history.

The march was historic for some other reasons, too. It created an atmosphere and an environment of sisterhood. And even though it wasn't without its own issues (see: organized largely by white women, leaving some women of color feeling left out of the narrative, and with some questions about antisemitism as well), it helped women feel prepped to stand together against sexism.

Which is to say: it made perfect sense that the #MeToo movement hit later that year. The atmosphere, the foundation, the energy was there. It had all been brewing for some time. And then came the bombshell.

From Aggressive Overtures to Sexual Assault: Harvey Weinstein's Accusers Tell Their Stories (*The New Yorker*)

It was the article heard around the world.

Before long, eighty-seven women were pointing fingers at Harvey Weinstein—one of the biggest producers in the entertainment industry—for sexual misconduct and sexual assault, including rape. Eighty-seven. Some of those women included Amber Anderson, Kate Beckinsale, Asia Argento, Cara Delevingne, Salma Hayek, Angelina Jolie, Rose McGowan, Lupita Nyong'o, and Gwyneth Paltrow. But there were countless others who alleged they had been harassed or assaulted by Weinstein, too.

The common thread? Weinstein used his position of power to get what he wanted—and ruined careers if he didn't.

These accusations started a movement.

People all over the world voiced their support for the women speaking out about Weinstein's actions. One such person was actor Alyssa Milano, whose tweet you'll see when you turn the page.

By the end of the day, #MeToo had been tweeted more than two hundred thousand times. On Facebook, it was used by more than 4.7 million people in twelve million posts during the first twenty-four hours.

Jaw, dropped.

More and more women kept coming forward. And they named names. More than two hundred of those names belonged to very, very powerful men.

Alyssa Milano ✔ @Alyssa_Milano · Oct 15, 2017 ···
If you've been sexually harassed or assaulted write 'me too' as a reply to this tweet.

> Me too.
>
> Suggested by a friend: "If all the women who have been sexually harassed or assaulted wrote 'Me too.' as a status, we might give people a sense of the magnitude of the problem."

🗨 61K   ⇄ 38.6K   ♡ 48.8K   ⬆

Alyssa Milano ✔ @Alyssa_Milano · Oct 15, 2017 ···
Me too.

🗨 1.2K   ⇄ 898   ♡ 5.1K   ⬆

And people began facing consequences.

Louis C.K. Is Accused by 5 Women of Sexual Misconduct
(*The New York Times*)

Louis CK Cancelled by Everyone (VICE News)

Kevin Spacey Scandal: A Complete List of the 15 Accusers (*USA Today*)

House of Cards Returns without Kevin Spacey Heading the Cast (*The Guardian*)

Eight Women Say Charlie Rose Sexually Harassed Them—with Nudity, Groping and Lewd Calls
(*The Washington Post*)

Charlie Rose Fired by CBS and PBS after Harassment Allegations (*The New York Times*)

Matt Lauer Accused of Sexual Harassment by Multiple Women (*Variety*)

NBC News Fires Matt Lauer after Sexual Misconduct Review (NBC News)

Harvey Weinstein Sentenced to 23 Years in Jail
(BBC News)

ICYMI, it's not often that women (or men, or anyone else) who are sexually assaulted get justice. According to the US Justice Dept, 63 percent of sexual assaults are never reported to police. And the assaults that *do* get reported rarely result in a conviction. Even if they do, the sentences can be startlingly low. (See: Brock Turner, who raped Chanel Miller, an unconscious, intoxicated woman—and got six months in county jail. He only ended up serving three of those months.)

Plus there's this little thing called victim blaming.

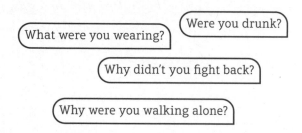

Those are all prime examples of victim blaming. Think: the idea that the victim of sexual assault was, you know, "asking for it."

#MeToo gave victims a voice. It gave victims a community to stand up with against their abusers. And the effect of aaaall those accusations coming out in such a short span of time led to some real justice—for once.

It didn't just change things for victims. It changed things for women in so many places. Suddenly, people were talking about revamping the entertainment industry to make it safer for women—and similar conversations were happening in other industries, too. People were having conversations about sexual assault in a way that made it less taboo. People were speaking up when sexual misconduct occurred—and educating others on what that looks like. (Of course, the problem is still definitely not solved, but #MeToo was a huge step in the right direction.)

And to think—all because of a hashtag. Or rather, how people were able to *use* a hashtag to make a difference.

That's a pretty powerful thing.

Immigration, DACA, and Dreamers

I mentioned Trump a bit in connection with the #MeToo movement, so let's talk about something else that's often connected with the former prez: immigration—or, more specifically, undocumented immigration. That's when immigrants enter the US illegally. And ICYMI, it was a big part of why Trump went on to win the presidency.

Remember xenophobia? If you've been able to spot it throughout this book, that's great. (Well, the xenophobia isn't great, but you know what I mean.) Xenophobia comes back into play here. In 2016, xenophobia was just as strong as ever in the US, so when Trump went around declaring that immigrants coming across the US–Mexico border were stealing Americans' jobs, were not paying taxes, and were even straight-up "rapists and murderers," millions of Americans were all too ready to listen.

He offered up solutions. BUILD A WALL! DEFUND SANCTUARY CITIES! INCREASE BORDER SECURITY!

. . . REPEAL DACA!

DACA stands for Deferred Action for Childhood Arrivals. Prez Barack Obama intro'd the law to protect migrants brought to the United States illegally as kids—since, you know, they didn't exactly have any say in the matter. Most of the young people protected under DACA (known as Dreamers) have spent most of their lives in the US, but still don't have citizenship. DACA basically keeps these kids from being deported.

There are currently about seven hundred thousand Dreamers living in the United States—and some estimates put the number as high as eight hundred thousand. The average age of a Dreamer is twenty-four years old, with two-thirds of Dreamers being under the age of twenty-five. In other words: Gen Zers.

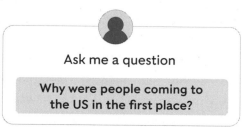

A wide variety of reasons. People were coming because of every-thing from the threat of persecution and violence in their home countries to extreme poverty—or just generally wanting to make a better life for themselves and their families. (Side note: if an immigrant has a serious fear of persecution or some other kind of danger, they can be granted asylum in the United States, even if they've crossed the border illegally.)

You're right—the US could totally do more to get to the root of the problem and hand aid or other forms of help to the countries most impacted by these issues. And they do. But the money is either not enough or just not helpful, and plenty of issues exist beyond US control. (Not to mention some of these conditions exist in the first place due to past US interference in Latin American politics.)

Ask me a question

What were Trump's thoughts on DACA?

In case that wasn't clear . . . he was not a fan. At all. In fact, in 2017, he officially ended the program.

Ask me a question

What was the response?

The decision was instantly met with backlash from critics—especially people protected under DACA.

But it was also met with lots of praise from supporters, who see Dreamers as a drain on US resources.

So yeah. Cue protests, which broke out across the country and brought out huge crowds in support of DACA.

People didn't just protest.

They also sued.

15 States, D.C. Sue to Stop Trump DACA Decision
(NBC News)

Six Dreamers Sue Trump Administration over DACA Decision (Reuters)

There's a catch to this whole story. Prez Trump didn't just end DACA; he also gave Congress a few short months to figure out a replacement plan.

The lives of hundreds of thousands of Dreamers were hanging in the balance.

After months of debates and delayed deadlines, Congress stiiiill couldn't figure things out. And all this time, while current Dreamers were technically protected, no one could renew this protection. Plus no new applications were being accepted.

Ask me a question

Wait . . . What happened with the lawsuits?

I was just about to get back to that. This whole time, the lawsuits were slowly making their way aaaaall the way up to the Supreme Court.

Finally, in June 2020, SCOTUS made its ruling.

But let's backtrack for a second. The Supreme Court has nine judges—called justices. Each justice is nominated by whatever prez is in office when a vacancy comes up, so the Supreme Court can sometimes lean either more liberal or more conservative, depending on which recent prezes have been able to nominate more justices.

By this point in his presidency, Trump had gotten the chance to nominate two justices to the Supreme Court—tipping the balance squarely in Republicans' favor, and, thus, in Trump's. So everyone was pretty much expecting the Supremes to vote against DACA.

Cue even more suspense.

On the day of the decision, people nationwide were staring at their phones, waiting to hear Dreamers' fate.

Then . . . the gavel came down.

A: omg. the supreme court ruled daca can stay.

B: really?!

A: yes! the vote was 5-4. justice roberts sided with the liberal justices.

B: no way. trump's not going to be happy.

He wasn't. He pointed fingers at the Supremes for going against *him* on purpose. But it didn't matter.

DACA was saved.

. . . or not.

The Supreme Court left things a bit open ended. The justices said Trump's attempt to end DACA was unconstitutional because he didn't give a strong enough reason for doing so. Meaning if someone *was* able to come up with a good enough reason, DACA could hypothetically still be axed.

At the end of the day, one of the most important takeaways here is seeing just how directly politics affects people. And not just some people—a whole lot of them. In this case, seven hundred thousand.

In other words: the fates of the seven hundred thousand people protected under DACA are tied to the choices of the American public. As in, *you*. And they will continue to be for years to come. That's a straight-up fact—one that can't be ignored, whether you're for DACA or against it.

March for Our Lives

Flashback to the hippie movement and the Vietnam War protests. Remember how I said that was one of the first big youth-led protest movements?

Here's the second.

On February 14, 2018, a school shooting took place in Parkland, Florida. It wasn't the first school shooting that the US had seen—sadly, not in the slightest—but it changed the conversation about gun violence in a major way.

But before we get into the effects, let's go into what happened during the shooting itself, as told by the students who lived it. CNN got ahold of tweets from Aidan Minoff, who live tweeted the shooting from inside the school. Here's one:

> My school is being shot up and I am locked inside. I'm f***ing scared right now

In text messages obtained by *The Washington Post*, a group of friends checked in on each other and kept each other updated over the course of the shooting.

ARE ALL OF YOU OKAY

yes

Yes bb are you?

me and ---- are good

I'll look

physically yes

Every one stay safe

Just try to keep calm

7 people dead

i'm going to fucking vomit

carmen is in two of my classes

where did you hear that

oh my god

she's my friend

Here's another tweet from Aidan:

I am still locked in the school, but remember I'm only a freshman. Please don't just send your love to me, but pray for the victims' families too. Love you all.

And back to the group of friends:

> someone's cuffed and being put in the car

> is everyone still okay

> yes

> yes

Aidan's tweets continued:

> We have been liberated

> You may never know when it may be the last day you meet someone

At the end of the day, seventeen people had been killed. Nikolas Cruz, who was responsible for the shooting, was in custody. And the lives of the students of Marjory Stoneman Douglas High would never be the same.

Meet Emma González, a senior at MSD. Like many of their peers, they were outraged by the laws that had allowed Cruz to obtain a gun and use it to kill their classmates. (This sort of outrage wasn't new by any means, BTW. For years, there had been organizations fighting for gun control, many of which were established after other school shootings. Think: Columbine and Sandy Hook, among others.) So just days after the shooting, they spoke at a gun control rally in their town.

Little did they know, there were CNN cameras there.

 The people in the government who were voted into power are lying to us. And us kids seem to be the only ones who notice and our parents to call BS. Companies trying to make

caricatures of the teenagers these days, saying that all we are self-involved and trend-obsessed and they hush us into submission when our message doesn't reach the ears of the nation, we are prepared to call BS. Politicians who sit in their gilded House and Senate seats funded by the NRA telling us nothing could have been done to prevent this, we call BS. They say tougher gun laws do not decrease gun violence. We call BS. They say a good guy with a gun stops a bad guy with a gun. We call BS. They say guns are just tools like knives and are as dangerous as cars. We call BS. They say no laws could have prevented the hundreds of senseless tragedies that have occurred. We call BS. That us kids don't know what we're talking about, that we're too young to understand how the government works. We call BS. 🙽

The speech went viral—as did Emma González.

Just like that, the (budding) movement had a face.

And not just one face. A day before González gave her speech, Cameron Kasky, also a senior at MSD, took to Facebook:

Can't sleep. Thinking about so many things. So angry that I'm not scared or nervous anymore ... I'm just angry. I just want people to understand what happened and understand that doing nothing will lead to nothing. Who'd have thought that concept was so difficult to grasp?

That post got him media attention. It didn't take him long to realize that all of the US was listening to the students of MSD—at least for a moment. And that wasn't a moment he was going to waste.

So Kasky invited a few friends over. They pulled an all-nighter creating social media accounts and thinking up a platform.

Their demands?

Pass a law to ban assault weapons.
Stop the sale of high-capacity magazines.
Implement laws that require background checks on aaaaall gun purchases, including online and at gun shows.

Over the coming days, Kasky got more and more students on board. He approached González after her viral speech. He approached David Hogg, an MSD school newspaper reporter, after he demanded action from elected officials on TV. He approached Sarah Chadwick after she tweeted at Prez Trump. He approached Jaclyn Corin after she started chatting with state reps to make plans to bus a hundred MSD students to Washington, DC, to talk gun control.

This organization became known as Never Again MSD.

Together, the students had an idea. They decided to plan a march.

A march that would raise awareness about what had happened at Marjory Stoneman Douglas High School. A march that would get students all across the country involved. A march for laws that would ensure the Parkland school shooting was the very last. A march for gun control. A March for Our Lives.

The date of the march was set. The students of Never Again MSD knew their window to make an impact was rapidly narrowing and did everything they could to keep up the media attention. They said yes to practically every media request. They went forward with that lobbying day in Washington, DC. They had a listening session with Prez Trump. They got the support of countless celebrities.

Just over a month after Nikolas Cruz took seventeen lives . . . the day of the march arrived.

March 24, 2018

There were marches all across the country, but the main march was in Washington, DC. There, student activists grabbed the mic for speeches that were heard around the country.

Emma González held a moment of silence. A six-minute-and-twenty-second moment, to be exact—the same amount of time as the shooting. David Hogg got political and made it clear the students of MSD would be holding politicians accountable. Then added that he didn't want "thoughts and prayers"—he wanted action. Eleven-year-old

Naomi Wadler drew attention to the fact that Black women and girls are often the victims of gun violence, but don't always make the front page of the news. Yolanda Renee King, the granddaughter of Martin Luther King Jr., had a dream that "enough is enough"—a big rallying cry for the movement. Alex King and D'Angelo McDade came on stage with duct tape over their mouths and spoke about the importance of nonviolence. Cameron Kasky pledged to build a better world.

By the end of the day, at least 1.2 million people had taken part in marches nationwide.

Hundreds of marches had been organized.

The march in Washington, DC, was one of the biggest gun control rallies—ever.

And March for Our Lives as a whole? Well, it was one of the biggest youth protests since the Vietnam War and the hippie movement—if not *the* biggest.

For the first time, people saw a real hope of creating change when it came to gun control laws. For some context: the US has this little thing called the Second Amendment, which basically says that any American has the "right to bear arms." In other words: own a gun. People take that amendment very seriously, especially since organizations like the National Rifle Association spend lots of time and money lobbying politicians.

So, long story short . . . there were endless roadblocks to gun control laws. Endless groups of people trying to knock down activists who were inching the tug-of-war rope closer and closer to their side.

March for Our Lives started to chip away at those roadblocks, gather more people to grab the rope . . . and begin tugging.

Florida Gov. Rick Scott Breaks with NRA to Sign New Gun Regulations (*The Washington Post*)

Trump Administration Imposes Ban on Bump Stocks (*The New York Times*)

House Passes Bill to Improve School Safety in Wake of Parkland Shooting (CBS News)

Walmart Announces It Will No Longer Sell Guns, Ammunition to Anyone Under 21 (NPR)

Dick's Sporting Goods Will Stop Selling Assault-Style Rifles (NBC News)

But the students of Never Again MSD—and the students who had joined or even started gun control groups across the country—still had a long way to go to reach their goals. The why: their demands still weren't being met on a federal level. Assault weapons have still not been banned. High-capacity magazines are still being sold. And background checks on aaaall gun purchases . . . are still not required. (Again, this is all on a federal level—some of these laws do exist on a more local level.)

This is the number of people killed or injured in school shootings since the Parkland school shooting (or at least, as of this writing). It's tragically high. But thanks to March for Our Lives, young people are continuing to fight for gun control.

March 2018:	**5** deaths, **7** injuries	June 2019:	**2, 11**
April 2018:	**0, 2**	July 2019:	**0, 1**
May 2018:	**11, 20**	August 2019:	**1, 12**
June 2018:	**0, 0**	Sept. 2019:	**1, 10**
July 2018:	**0, 0**	October 2019:	**1, 1**
August 2018:	**1, 3**	Nov. 2019:	**7, 7**
Sept. 2018:	**2, 2**	Dec. 2019:	**1, 5**
Oct. 2018:	**1, 1**	Jan. 2020:	**2, 5**
Nov. 2018:	**0, 0**	Feb. 2020:	**2, 1**
Dec. 2018:	**1, 0**	None from March to August, and then in Sept. 2020:	**1, 1**
Jan. 2019:	**2, 8**	None from October to January then in Feb. 2021:	**1, 0**
Feb. 2019:	**2, 2**	March 2021:	**1, 0**
March 2019:	**0, 3**	April 2021:	**1, 0**
April 2019:	**0, 3**	May 2021:	**0, 3**
May 2019:	**2, 18**		

Not only that, but March for Our Lives exposed millions more young people to the idea of youth activism. It successfully amplified and brought into the mainstream the power of young people to create change, on a scale not seen in recent years.

Because of March for Our Lives, making change as a member of Generation Z (that's us!) seemed much more accessible than ever before. Because of March for Our Lives, Gen Z had a collective platform. A collective voice.

And it would set the stage for many more youth activists to come . . .

The Climate Change Movement

When you think youth activism, chances are climate change is one of the first things that comes to mind. But before we really get into the climate change movement, it's important to fully understand just what climate change is and how it's affecting our world.

The Causes

ICYMI, we all basically live in one big greenhouse. That's what allows us (and all life on Earth) to survive. Our atmosphere (the transparent roof of the greenhouse) absorbs heat from the sun—which is a good thing, to be super clear, since it's what keeps our planet from succumbing to the frozen vacuum of space. What's not good is that the heat then radiates back up in the form of infrared light, about 90 percent of which is reabsorbed by greenhouse gases in our atmosphere (like carbon dioxide, methane, nitrous oxide, and water vapor) . . . and reflected right back toward Earth's surface, in the form of more heat. It's sort of like the planet is wearing a sweater in 70-degree weather, and then layers on another sweater, and then a windbreaker, and then a parka, and then a blanket . . . It's overkill. It's dangerous. And it causes weird things to happen.

Okay, fine, you say. That's been happening for forever—but

climate change hasn't been happening for forever. This greenhouse effect started becoming a big problem over the last several decades as the world changed rapidly and drastically. Everything from cars (because, more carbon dioxide) to Big Macs (because, more methane from cows) contributes to the greenhouse effect. And not in a positive way.

More greenhouse gases means more heat is reflected back toward Earth's surface. Which leads the whole world to get a whole lot hotter. See above: weird things start to happen.

So, definitely a problem.

The Effects

A hotter planet has all kinds of ramifications. First, the weather. Yeah, duh. But extreme heat waves can lead to problems in almost every aspect of life, from work (think of farmers, for example) to health. And not only that, but hotter global temps lead to more extreme disasters, like more intense hurricanes, floods, and wildfires—and even more heavy snowfall. Plus rising sea levels.

Think of the implications of that. In the United States alone, 127 million people live by the coast. Some of our biggest cities—New York, Los Angeles, San Francisco, New Orleans, Miami, Houston, Boston, the list goes on—are on the water. And research shows more than half of those cities could be almost totally destroyed by 2100. And again, that's just in the US. Other parts of the world would see even more dramatic changes to coastal areas.

There would be a mass migration. Mass job loss. Mass homelessness. Mass starvation.

Or worse—mass death.

People wouldn't be the only ones affected if we don't stop climate change. Plants and animals both on and off land would be under threat. Some estimates say half of all wildlife habitats would be lost.

And what's horrible is that a lot of this stuff is already happening.

It's a very real and present danger. (But you'll read more about all of that in just a few pages.)

To sum things up: our world would be changed—and, in fact, is already changing. Irreversibly.

The Solutions

Staving off a disaster that would change our world in such a dramatic way would require some changes to our society. These changes would serve to fight climate change, yes, but they'd also lead to a better society in general. You'll see what I mean.

Cutting out fossil fuels and replacing them with cleaner energy sources. Investing in more sustainable infrastructure and eco-friendly transportation. Consuming less of, well, everything. Making more conscious choices to positively impact the environment as we go about our lives. Switching up farming tactics to be more considerate of the ecological impact (so that's a no on deforestation, among other things). Leaving old-growth forests untouched and protected. Planting trees to absorb gases.

All of these things can help keep temps from continuing to rise—and hopefully keep our world from being overtaken by climate change.

Only a slight problem . . . world leaders haven't exactly taken climate change—or the above solutions—all that seriously. Or even if they have (hint: the Paris climate agreement), it's been seen as far too little.

Enter: climate activism.

This idea of fighting for the environment has been around for a long while. See: Earth Day, marches, protests, and policies for the environment in the 1970s—not to mention lots of the aforementioned solutions were created decades ago, before climate change even went mainstream.

In fact, Native American communities in particular have been tirelessly (and often thanklessly) fighting against climate change and drivers of climate change for longer than pretty much anyone else (the Dakota Access pipeline and Keystone XL pipeline, anyone?). And it's communities like those (along with people of color in general) who would likely be most impacted by climate change.

And really, already are being more impacted by climate change.

Remember redlining? The effects of that very racist practice that controlled where people of color could live are still being felt today. Formerly redlined neighborhoods typically have fewer trees, parks, and overall greenery compared to not-redlined (and predominantly white) neighborhoods. Which causes land prices to stay low. Meaning a lot of that land is now used for things like highways, warehouses, power plants, garbage dumps, new industries, and public housing.

The upshot: Formerly redlined areas have less greenery and more pavement. Less greenery and more pavement = higher temps, worse air quality, problematic infrastructure that doesn't mitigate the effects of climate change . . . and more health problems.

All of the above is a really good example of why it's important to remember that for a lot of youth climate activists, they don't have the choice or the privilege to decide whether to get involved. It's a matter of life and death right this very instant.

So yes. Youth climate activism has been around for a good amount of time. But it didn't really begin getting the kind of media attention it deserved until a young woman named—you guessed it—Greta Thunberg had an idea.

You likely know the story.

How Thunberg went into a state of depression upon finding out about climate change when she was a young(er) girl. How she finally decided to go on strike from school every Friday (known as Fridays for Future) in 2018 to raise awareness for climate change. How the story went viral. How Thunberg went on to speak before countless world leaders about the failures of our leadership and the need to take action so Gen Z isn't left with a ruined world.

It wasn't long before Thunberg's message and method of protest had caught on among other young people.

By other, I mean well over one million young people. All. Over. The. World.

And young people are still protesting. Young people are still fighting to find solutions, to lobby the gov, to hold bizes accountable. Because we've now seen, more than ever before, that one young person can raise her voice . . . and a million more will answer.

Climate change and social justice have now become part of the heart of Gen Z's activism. After all, our generation is the one that's going to have to face the brunt of the consequences of climate change. We of all people know just how urgent a disaster this is. Older generations have given us no choice but to do everything we can to fight to prevent it from doing further damage.

It's up to us. (That's Sad but True Facts, brought to you by *Cramm This Book*.)

So if March for Our Lives intro'd the idea of youth activism on a modern scale, climate activism solidified it. After Fridays for Future, it was clearer than ever before that youth activism was not and is not a trend. It's a defining aspect of Gen Z. It's a common thread that ties us together. And it just might be the thing that saves us all.

Climate change is by no means a solved problem. Nor is it one that's in the distant future. Communities today are being ravaged by the effects of climate change, and it's critical that we keep up the fight to solve it.

Because if we don't? The repercussions can be catastrophic and deadly.

But if we do? We just might save the world. Literally.

THE DISASTERS

In the chapter at the end of the last section, I talked about climate activism and why it's so important. I also referenced some of the disasters that climate change has brought about. Now it's time to get specific about those disasters and a whole bunch of others. As you look at the collection of disasters that have come about in relatively recent history, you'll see that they often fall into a few key categories: oil spills, nuclear meltdowns and explosions, money issues, hurricanes, fires, and disease-related disasters. And not to give away the point of this all, but there's a strong human element to all of these disasters, whether you realize it or not.

You're about to read about some of the biggest disasters that have occurred over the past half a century or so. Like everything in this book, there's a set of very specific reasons why I included these particular disasters. Hint: every single one of these disasters changed the world. Significantly.

You'll see what I mean. Read on.

Oil Spills

1969. Santa Barbara, California. You head to the beach, excited to spend the day with your friends. You walk up, feeling the sand between your toes, the sun on your face, the breeze on your skin . . .

And then you stop short.

The ocean is a deep, dark, opaque black. It looks as if the water has been poisoned. The beach is thick with what looks like pools of sticky black sand. You start wrinkling your nose; the air smells pungent, almost like everything has been recently repaved—you know, just like a street with a fresh coat of tar.

That's when it dawns on you.

It's oil.

Everywhere.

It stretches for dozens of miles. It leaches the life from the beach and from the ocean. Literally. It's impossible not to spot a bird trapped within the oppressive tar. You also see the corpses of marine life tossed up on shore with the blackened waves.

There are people at the beach, too, dressed in yellow and wearing tall boots. They are freeing birds and using shovels to clear what seems like endless amounts of oil.

Your mind settles on a solo, painful thought: one oil spill caused this. One oil spill single-handedly transformed the beach from a beautiful expanse of nature to a disaster zone.

Thirty-five hundred sea birds were ultimately killed—as were countless other marine animals, like dolphins and elephant seals and sea lions. In total, an estimated three million gallons of crude oil went straight into the ocean. It was the worst oil spill in United States history. (Well. At the time.)

And all because a biz called Unocal (then known as Union Oil) didn't take the proper safety precautions.

This one oil spill also did something else astronomically significant.

It, in part, launched the environmental movement.

The idea of environmental conservation had been around before, sure. But large groups of people had yet to really take up the cause.

This time was different. The nation was spurred by the images of ruined beaches and dead animals. People started organizing citizen-led environmental groups. This little thing called Earth Day was created. A long list of new laws and regulations were intro'd, all with the goal of protecting the environment and ensuring something like this never happened again.

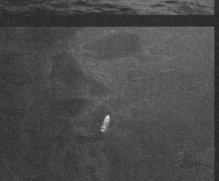

Spoiler alert: it still did.

Here are just a few of the oil spills that happened over the next few decades:

Japan Fighting Her Biggest Oil Spill
(*The New York Times*, 1974)

Wreck of the Amoco Cadiz Revives Issue of Safety in Transporting Oil (*The New York Times*, 1978)

Mexican Oil Spill Continues, Still Baffling the Experts
(*The New York Times*, 1979)

Major Damage Feared in Persian Gulf Oil Spill
(*The New York Times*, 1983)

Ship Breaks Up off Cape Town, Sending Oil Spill toward Beaches (*Associated Press*, 1983)

Exxon Oil Spill Devastated a Way of Life
(*The New York Times*, 1994)

Russians Struggle to Clean Up Spill
(*The New York Times*, 1994)

[Deepwater Horizon] Gulf Spill Is the Largest of Its Kind, Scientists Say (*The New York Times*, 2010)

Let's take a closer look at that last one. On the night of April 20, 2010, a whole lot of natural gas burst through a concrete core that was installed by Halliburton (you might remember that as the biz former vice prez Dick Cheney used to lead) to seal an oil well in the Gulf of Mexico. The well was located beneath an oil rig called Deepwater Horizon, owned and operated by Transocean and leased by oil biz BP.

The natural gas kept traveling up to the rig's platform.

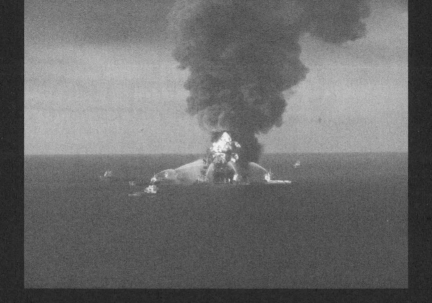

It ignited.

It killed eleven workers and injured seventeen.

And the disaster didn't stop there.

The rig capsized. Sank. The effect? Oil began seeping from the well into the ocean.

It. Just. Kept. Going.

Soon, the ocean was transformed.

Forty-one years after the 1969 Santa Barbara oil spill, the United States was yet again facing its largest-ever oil spill. Not only that, but it was the largest marine oil spill in history.

An estimated 3.19 million barrels of oil leaked into the Gulf of Mexico.

That's 130 million gallons of oil.

130 million.

But out of every darkness comes light.

As with the 1969 Santa Barbara oil spill, Deepwater Horizon woke the United States up to just how destructive of an impact these oil spills can have on the environment.

Cue the most aggressive reforms to things like offshore oil and gas regulation and oversight in US history. Think: the gov restructured the Minerals Management Service, which is in charge of federal oil and gas leasing, to address a long list of conflicts of interest that were keeping the agency from properly doing its job. Plus the gov changed liability requirements for those who work in the oil and gas drilling space. Add those two examples to the countless other reforms that were passed, and the US's environmental policy was suddenly looking a whole lot different. (But it's also very important to note that these reforms can be trashed just as easily—and some already have been—so it's up to us to stay up to date with politics and use our voices for change if it needs to be made.)

The changes that were put in place after the Deepwater Horizon spill were a very big deal. Because those reforms held bizes accountable. They helped increase workplace safety. They put in place safety requirements for well designs. They did all sorts of things that created a lasting impact on the oil industry.

Because, to this day, oil spills, big or small, are not as rare as we'd like to think. Unocal and Deepwater Horizon—along with the others that I referenced in the headlines above—were a couple of the most devastating oil spills, but they certainly weren't the only ones. Oil spills continue to happen, and they continue to harm the environment.

As long as people keep using oil, our planet will keep being affected.

But the good news? We get to decide what those effects look like.

This story isn't over yet.

And we have the power to finish it.

Nuclear Meltdowns and Explosions

You probably associate the word "nuclear" with things like the Cold War and weapons of mass destruction. But much of the world's energy (read: 10 percent of all electricity) actually comes from nuclear energy.

If you're wondering what that is, here's the short-form version. Nuclear energy basically comes from splitting atoms in a reactor, which heats water into steam, turns a turbine, and—voilà!—generates electricity. Simple.

But there are some problems. Like, a lot. Aside from typical logistical things (like cost and time), there are concerns that countries that import uranium for use in nuclear energy facilities could then secretly start using it to build nuclear weapons. A political and diplomatic nightmare, BTW. Then there are the health risks. See: you need uranium for nuclear energy—and mining for uranium can lead to lung cancer. Plus there are the risks of meltdown (caused by a malfunctioning reactor) and the ever-present question of where to store used-up fuel rods from nuclear plants (basically what we call radioactive waste, which gives off radioactivity that is deadly for hundreds of thousands of years).

Not so simple.

Sometimes, those problems result in full-on disasters.

Those are the sites of some of the worst nuclear disasters in history. And the repercussions? Well, they're still being felt today.

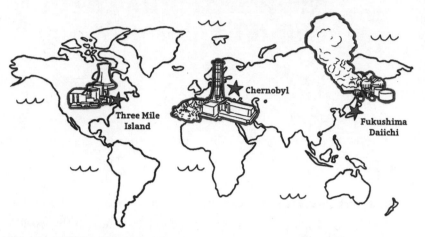

Three Mile Island, 1979

We'll start with Three Mile Island. Aka the worst accident in the history of the US nuclear power industry. Yes, really. Here's the story: in 1979, a pressure valve in a reactor didn't close . . . which led radiation-contaminated cooling water to drain into nearby buildings . . . which led the core to heat up. A lot. So emergency cooling pumps automatically kicked in.

Only a slight problem . . . the human operators in the control room got the tiniest bit confused due to some contradictory readings. And that tiniest bit of confusion caused them to make a massively dangerous mistake: shutting off the emergency system.

One thing led to another, and by morning, the core had heated to near-meltdown levels. ICYDK, a meltdown is basically the worst-case scenario for nuclear power plants, because it means that containment of the radioactive plutonium in the fuel rods is breached and deadly radiation leaks out into the world.

Thankfully, there wasn't a full-on nuclear meltdown here—more like what nuclear experts refer to as a "partial meltdown." There was a small explosion with a bubble of gas, which released radiation into the air. And even though it wasn't much, it was still majorly unhealthy. See: in the years since, it's led to all kinds of health problems, including increases in cancer, birth defects, autoimmune diseases, infertility, and more.

Cleanup took eleven years. Not a typo. The memories of the disaster lasted even longer. See: not a single new nuclear power plant has been built in the US since Three Mile Island.

But even Three Mile Island was far from the biggest nuclear disaster in the history of the whole world.

That would be Chernobyl.

Chernobyl, 1986

You've probably heard at least a little bit about Chernobyl. You know—the fast facts.

It took place in 1986. There was a steam explosion. Fires. All of that caused at least 5 percent of the radioactive reactor core to be unleashed upon the environment and throughout Europe. Two plant workers died due to the explosion. Twenty-eight more people (including firefighters) died over the next few weeks due to acute radiation syndrome. Over the following years, thousands upon thousands of people were diagnosed with thyroid cancer. And fifteen more people died as a result. 350,000 people were evacuated—and relocation efforts are ongoing.

Maybe you've heard bits and pieces of the above information. But what's reeeeally startling is just how inevitable it all was.

And, spoiler: it all goes back to the Cold War.

Let's go back to 1970. The Chernobyl nuclear power plant, which is located in Ukraine—at the time, part of the Soviet Union—starts getting built. About half of the power plant was finished in 1977.

It's not hard to understand why the Soviet Union was building a nuclear power plant. Aside from aaaall the energy it could offer, "nuclear" was pretty much the word of the decade. Both the US and the Soviet Union were looking to test the limits of nuclear power, whether it was with energy or with weapons.

But here's the thing: when research is conducted in isolation, you're more likely to face problems. In other words: the Soviets were building a nuclear power plant pretty much on their own, which made them more prone to mistakes. Add that to the fact that there weren't a whole lot of concerns about safety at the time, and you've got a full-blown disaster.

Literally.

There were a lot of flaws in how the plant was built. The operators were inexperienced. All sorts of rules were being broken—mostly because they hadn't even been written yet.

When the warning signs began popping up, people pressed the ignore button.

The results, as you've already read, were catastrophic.

It was another twenty-five years before the world saw another nuclear disaster on this scale.

Fukushima Daiichi, 2011

You've maybe also heard a little bit about Fukushima Daiichi—or maybe not. What makes this nuclear disaster so different from the other two I just mentioned is that (a) it is much more recent and (b) it wasn't really a result of incompetence or some massive flaw.

Which makes it all the more terrifying.

There are two ways to discuss Fukushima Daiichi, because really, it was more than just a nuclear disaster. It was an earthquake and a tsunami and a nuclear disaster all wrapped up into one. So you could either go through the complete timeline of everything that happened—as things got progressively worse and worse and the world realized the full gravity of the situation—or you could just give the gist.

Since this book is called *Cramm This Book*, I'll go with the second option.

I already mentioned the earthquake. The Fukushima Daiichi nuclear power plant had protocols in place for when something like an earthquake happens, so while an emergency was triggered, nobody was too, too freaked out.

But then the earthquake triggered a tsunami.

And that's when people started hitting the panic button.

Those protocols (which involved emergency diesel generators) stopped working, because there were just too many things failing at once. The protocols involved some temporary fixes that go into effect in case of emergency, but the key word here is "temporary"—and with everything going wrong at once, the temporary measures didn't last long.

At this point, all eyes are on the spent fuel pools in each of the six units at the nuclear power plant, because with everything going on, those were the known danger points.

ICYDK, those things are full of radiation. So you can probably imagine that they're very, very secure.

Exceeeept if there happens to be a hydrogen explosion or a fire.

Exceeeept if that hydrogen explosion or fire happens to damage enough of the building that the spent fuel pool is exposed to the atmosphere.

Exceeeept if the spent fuel pool boils, which would then release radiation into the atmosphere.

Those first two things happen. And not just to one of the six units—no, it happens to four of them.

Cue evacuations.

And more evacuations.

And more evacuations.

At this point, it's been over a week since the earthquake hit. Things start to get under control. Over the next few days, there are a couple of scares, but mostly, everything seems to go pretty well.

Not so fast. Because it turns out some radiation diiiiid escape. Word gets out: milk and spinach from areas near the Fukushima Daiichi plant have radiation levels that are higher than normal. So does water in the area.

So there's this feeling of both triumph and panic as the spent fuel pools cool down . . . but more and more reports come out about things being more radioactive than they previously were.

It's another eight or so months before Japanese prime minister Yoshihiko Noda announces that the reactors are in a stable state of cold shutdown.

But what's arguably the hardest work of all still lies ahead.

Because, hint: the area is still highly dangerous. All the remaining spent fuel from the spent fuel pools needs to be removed. So does the fuel debris from the damaged reactors.

That's a process that will take ten years. Ten. Years.

After that, the site needs to be decommissioned (or retired from service). Which will take another twenty to thirty years.

Take a second to think about that. That's a total of thirty or forty years of tireless work. Thirty or forty years of money spent, of labor. Thirty or forty years of an area being uninhabitable. Thirty or forty years before people can return home.

Thirty or forty years. All because of a few moments.

Here's the thing about nuclear power. It maybe gets some props for being a clean and green alternative to fossil fuels, and while that's not necessarily wrong, it forces us to compromise—cleaner energy for a not-as-safe future. Some argue that that compromise is worth it to save the planet, while others say that sustainable alternatives—like solar, wind, geothermal, tidal, hydro . . . to name a few—are much better options. The debate becomes even more heated when you consider that if all the money being poured into nuclear power (and the resulting cleanup if and when there's an explosion) is instead invested in those kinds of solutions, the need for a compromise evaporates entirely.

When it comes to our planet, why should we settle for anything less?

Recessions

Recession (noun): **a period of temporary economic decline during which trade and industrial activity are reduced, generally identified by a fall in GDP in two successive quarters**

If you pay any attention to the stock market or the economy, you know that it feels like almost every day that someone references "recessions."

For the record: GDP stands for gross domestic product. It's the monetary value of all goods and services made within a country within a certain time period, and it's kind of seen as a big indicator as to the size of an economy and its growth rate.

But recessions go beyond just facts and figures. They affect real people in very real ways.

CASE IN POINT

The Great Depression

Chances are you've heard about the Great Depression, too. We'll refresh your memory.

Stocks Lose 10 Billion in Day (*The Klamath News*)

Market Losses Reach New Level (*Harrisburg Telegraph*)

Stock Market to Close Friday and Saturday
(*The St. Louis Star*)

Stock Market Declares Recess (*The Springfield Leader*)

Stock Market in Severe Collapse (*Great Falls Tribune*)

Wall St. in Panic as Stocks Crash (*Brooklyn Daily Eagle*)

Unemployment Levels by Year	
1929:	3.2 percent
1930:	8.7 percent
1931:	15.9 percent
1932:	23.6 percent
1933:	24.9 percent

That's a lot of information. An overwhelming amount of information, even. But that's how it feels when you're living through a recession—a slow roll before all of a sudden, every alarm is going off and it's pretty much all you can hear.

This period of economic devastation lasted about ten years. The outcomes were pretty hugely significant.

If the Civil War was the biggest crisis in American history, in that it almost tore the country in two, then the Great Depression was the second-biggest crisis. Society appeared to be falling apart. That's because recessions aren't just about the economy—they exacerbate every other issue we face in society. Poor people become poorer, hungry people go hungrier, sick people become sicker . . .

People were out of work and out of hope.

But it's when things fall apart that we get the chance to rebuild them even better than they were before.

And that's just what people did in the aftermath of the Great Depression.

People wanted change. Maybe they didn't want Soviet

Union–level change, but there was a big bump in support for socialist and communist ideals.

Unions. Health insurance benefits. Social Security. Unemployment programs. Retirement benefits. Welfare. Stock market and bank regulation.

All the things I just listed out are practically the norm nowadays. But before the Great Depression, they either just didn't exist in American society or weren't popularized.

But through new policies, programs, projects, reforms, and regulations (like the New Deal—which today's Green New Deal directly references), all of the above slowly became an integral part of American society.

(And on the healthcare note: in the decades following the Great Depression, there were also big pushes to make universal healthcare a thing. Sound familiar?)

Looking back at the chaos of the time, one thing is absolutely clear: the US would not look even remotely like how it does today if the Great Depression hadn't happened.

1937–1938	You see that red there? That marks aaaall
1945	the times the US has hit a recession since the
1948–1949	Great Depression. About a dozen, to be exact.
1953–1954	But none have been as bad as the Great
1957–1958	Recession.
1960–1961	Dun dun dun.
1969–1970	
1973–1975	**December 2007**
1980	At first it was gradual. There were warning signs,
1981–1982	if you looked for them. Only, a slight problem . . .
1990–1991	no one *was* looking. By the time it was obvious, it
2001	was too late to go back and fix things.
2007–2009	Far too late.

A: oh my gosh. oh my gosh. oh my gosh. 8 MILLION PEOPLE are unemployed. 4 MILLION HOMES are getting foreclosed. there are literally foreclosure signs on every street in my neighborhood! 2.5 MILLION BUSINESSES are closing!

B: i know. it's horrible. they're calling it the great recession.

A: why is this happening?????

B: well, you know how banks used to only really give loans to people with good credit? eventually the housing market was doing so well that banks got kind of cocky and were like, hey, you have bad credit? here's a loan! buy a house, please!

A: okay, i'm confused. why would banks give loans to people with bad credit? isn't that like bad business?

B: oh totally. except banks decided to make interest reeeeeally expensive. people either didn't really understand or they didn't really care because house prices were going up so quickly that they basically figured they could sell their house in a couple years and turn a big profit.

A: gotcha. so . . . where did things go wrong?

B: the housing market can't be good forever, right? so once it started going down—and it went down super fast—not only could people no longer afford to pay their mortgages with the super-high interest, but they also couldn't even sell their houses to pay back the original loans because the value of their houses had sunk below what they'd originally paid for them. so banks foreclosed their homes and kicked people out. from there, there was just this spiral effect of everyone losing their jobs and not having enough money to buy things and businesses closing and the stock market crashing and . . . well, you get the idea. and the worst part is that every bank was making these bad loans, not just in america, but all. over. the. world.

A: whoa. what's going to happen?

B: idk. but the government is going to have to do SOMETHING or this will just keep getting worse and worse.

Our wise, totally real friend was right. The gov *did* do something. It stepped in and bailed out banks and big bizes (like General Motors) that were going bankrupt.

Saving banks and big bizes saved the economy.

The why: if banks are, well, bankrupt, they can't give loans—not just to normal, everyday people, but also to big bizes who rely on bank loans to run. And if some of the world's biggest bizes are bankrupt, a whole lot of people are going to be losing jobs.

Of course, bailing out banks and big bizes caused the national deficit (aka the difference between the amount of money the gov receives and the amount of money the gov spends) to spike. But as time went on and the US (and the world as a whole) began to recover from the Great Recession, the gov was paid back.

While that may sound like a smooth, easy fix, it wasn't. Lots of people were super opposed to the idea of the gov just handing money to private banks and other bizes. And it took years before the full impact of that decision really set in.

Even then, millions of Americans had suffered massive losses.

So that's what it means when people reference recessions. That's what people are afraid of.

The scariest part?

Recessions are incredibly unpredictable. You never quite know when one is looming on the horizon . . . and you never quite know just *what* the effects will continue to be years later.

But what we *do* know is that we have the ability to prevent recessions—or at least lessen the impact. Thanks to policies and regulations like the New Deal, we can ensure that more people will be protected—financially and otherwise—regardless of which way the economy sways.

Though it may sound dry, that's why it's especially important to pay close attention to the kinds of policies that are being passed . . . and the kinds of policies that are being repealed. Because it's really not just about money.

It's about basic human rights, whether it's healthcare or welfare. And it's up to us to make sure there are policies in place to ensure a more secure future for everyone.

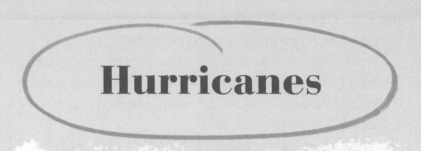

Hurricanes

Hurricane (noun): **a storm with a violent wind, in particular a tropical cyclone**

To elaborate—a tropical cyclone is a rotating weather system. Some key traits: hurricanes are low pressure, they have organized thunderstorms, and they have sustained winds of at least seventy-four miles per hour. There isn't a difference between hurricanes, cyclones, and typhoons—they're just called different things in different parts of the world.

Here's the other thing about hurricanes.

They have the potential to do massive, city-shattering, deadly damage.

Hurricanes are undoubtedly one of the most devastating types of disasters, wreaking havoc as they go. But what's often worse is the aftermath.

Don't believe me? Read on.

You will.

Hurricane Katrina (2005)

You might have heard of Hurricane Katrina as one of the worst storms the US has ever seen. But what made it quite so terrible? Let's take a look at what happened in August 2005 . . .

By the time the hurricane made its final landfall in Mississippi,

New Orleans

Superdome

Hurricane Katrina

countless lives had been lost. Countless buildings had been destroyed. But the real devastation had yet to come.

If you weren't aware, much of the area around New Orleans is below sea level. Think: between five and ten feet below sea level—and constantly sinking by about a centimeter per year. So you can probably imagine how easy it is for an area like this to flood.

Which is why, when Hurricane Katrina juuuuust missed New Orleans, the people of the city pretty much believed they had dodged a bullet.

Except they hadn't.

Because the city is so prone to floods, it's protected by levees and floodwalls. Turns out, those levees and floodwalls had some fundamental design flaws.

That's where everything went wrong.

An hour before the storm struck the Gulf Coast, the US Army Corps of Engineers got a report: the levees of New Orleans's largest drainage canal had been breached.

The other levees weren't doing much better. They were battling gigantic storm surges from the hurricane. And they were on the verge of losing those battles.

Over the course of the storm, more and more levees and flood-walls fell. In total, more than fifty locations lost that crucial protection.

Eighty percent of New Orleans flooded.

Ninety-five percent of Saint Bernard Parish, a nearby area, flooded.

Water reached depths of fifteen feet in some places.

One hundred thousand people were left stranded in New Orleans. One. Hundred. Thousand.

Then there were the power outages and transportation failures.

Both of those things served to make it that much harder to reach those in need.

Some people were trapped on roofs or in attics for days.

Tens of thousands evacuated to the Louisiana Superdome, where supplies quickly began running out.

Others weren't so lucky as to find high ground. It's estimated that more than 1,800 people died.

Even today, twelve thousand people are homeless in New Orleans as a result of Hurricane Katrina.

And here's one of the worst parts: for days, it felt like then prez

George W. Bush (and a whole slew of other gov officials) was largely ignoring it. When aid finally arrived, many people saw it as too little, too late.

I'll clue you in: much of the affected population was Black. And according to Pew research conducted a week after Katrina made landfall, many of the city's Black residents believed the gov's response would have been faster—*better*—if most of the victims had been white. They saw Katrina as revealing just how prevalent racial inequality still is in the United States.

That didn't mark the last time hurricane responses brought up conversations about race and inequality. Not sure what I mean? Read the rest of this chapter and find out.

Hurricane Ike (2008) and Hurricane Matthew (2016)

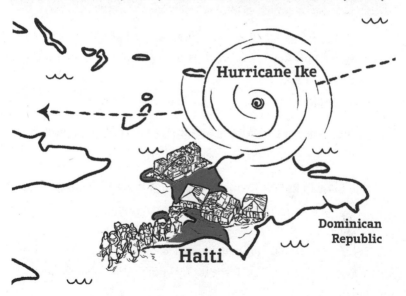

Hurricane Ike was one of those hurricanes that just kept coming back for more. It made landfall on the island of Great Inagua . . . then slammed into the Cuban coast . . . then intensified into a Category 2 . . . and made landfall once again near Galveston, Texas. The storm was so big that its effects were even felt in Canada. Wherever Ike went, intense flooding followed, bringing devastation to countless places.

Including Haiti.

ICYDK, Haiti had been hit with three major hurricanes in the three weeks preceding Ike. So the country was in bad shape to begin with. Hurricane Ike was the breaking point.

Seventy-four people died. Not only that, but after being hit with four massive hurricanes in a row, as many as one million Haitians were left homeless.

Even worse: relief was excruciatingly slow to come.

Haiti: Unanswered Needs in Gonaïves after Hurricanes
(Doctors Without Borders)

Aid Slow to Reach Towns in Haiti That Were Slammed by Hurricane (*The Washington Post*)

Before you think, *Oh, that happened over a decade ago*—think again. Because in 2016, Haiti was hit by yet another majorly destructive hurricane: Matthew.

The hurricane struck southwestern Haiti as a Category 5—marking it as the first Category 5 hurricane in the Atlantic since 2007. The effects were catastrophic, especially since the storm weakened, which caused it to slow and stick around longer. As a result,

90 percent of southern Haiti was destroyed and as many as 1,500 people were killed. The storm also served to worsen the country's already bad cholera outbreak and the continuing humanitarian crisis that stuck around after an earthquake in 2010.

By the time the hurricane had moved past Haiti, the country was facing a full-blown humanitarian disaster—cementing its reputation as one of the most natural-disaster-prone areas in the world.

It is also the poorest nation in the Western Hemisphere.

The poverty rate is between 59 and 65 percent to this day, with almost one in four Haitians living in extreme poverty. Some of the causes go all the way back to American occupation and colonialism, but these hurricanes—made increasingly worse by climate change—continue to keep the country from getting back on its feet.

Okay. Keep in mind what you just read and the takeaway—that the people often most impacted by hurricanes are BIPOC or low income—as we move on to this next hurricane: Hurricane Sandy, one of the deadliest, costliest hurricanes in US history.

Hurricane Sandy (2012)

Like Ike, Sandy made landfall multiple times, first in Jamaica, then Cuba, and finally near Atlantic City, New Jersey. The timing couldn't have been worse. The night Sandy hit, there was a full moon, which made high tides 20 percent higher than average. Cue an even bigger storm surge (aka a rising of water over a quick period of time).

Streets flooded. Trees and power lines were destroyed. Buildings caught on fire. People were left stranded.

Sandy didn't stop there. It made its way to Lower Manhattan,

causing seawater to crash into low-lying streets. Water got everywhere: tunnels, subway stations, electrical systems. And the wind. The wind made skyscrapers sway and forced a tanker ship into Staten Island.

Many people who could afford to leave fled before Sandy hit. They left the city in droves by car, spending the night at hotels far outside the city. Of those who didn't leave, the most financially stable were able to ask for time off work so they could stay home and hunker down.

But there were many thousands of people who simply couldn't ditch the city or their jobs, and who were forced squarely into the storm's path. Some people even slept in their cars. Yet again, this hurricane was most brutal for those who couldn't afford it.

In total, after Hurricane Sandy had swept across half the hemisphere, 285 people had died, with 125 of those deaths in the US. And the damage? It cost $65 billion (yes, with a *b*). It took years of cleanup. Thousands of people were displaced. People lost their homes, their

bizes, their livelihoods. Far too many people lost everything. And that's not something that just goes away as the waters recede.

Hurricane Sandy was soon surpassed in costliness by two other hurricanes, both of which took place in 2017.

Hurricane Harvey (2017)

I'll start with Hurricane Harvey.

Toward the end of summer 2017, Hurricane Harvey, a Category 4 storm, slammed into Texas and caused flash floods that authorities described as being "beyond anything experienced." Seriously. The flooding turned streets into rivers and partially submerged buildings.

Thousands of people had to be rescued. Ultimately, Harvey touched down in multiple other states throughout the South, leading to sixty-eight deaths (and another thirty-five deaths that were indirectly connected to the storm).

Within a month, Prez Donald Trump had taken a trip to Texas. More than $1.5 billion in federal funds were handed to Texans impacted by the disaster by way of assistance grants, low-interest disaster loans, flood insurance advance payments . . . to name a few.

Point being: as far as gov is concerned, the relief was pretty much instantaneous—which is great.

But keep that response in mind for this next hurricane.

Hurricane Maria (2017)

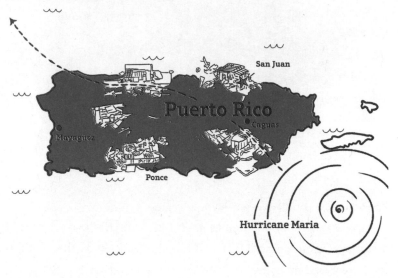

About a month later, Hurricane Maria, a near–Category 5 hurricane, became the strongest storm to hit Puerto Rico (a US territory, BTW) in nearly a century.

I'll repeat: Hurricane Maria was the strongest storm to hit Puerto Rico, which faces a looooot of storms, in nearly a century.

It made landfall with 155-mile-per-hour winds. Two-thirds of the island

dealt with direct impact. Thousands of people evacuated to shelters, with authorities getting hundreds of rescue calls. One hundred percent of the island's power grid was totally wiped out. Many towns were completely blocked off by huge mudslides.

At the time, officials said Puerto Ricans were likely to wake up to find the island totally destroyed.

The US gov at the time saw things a little . . . differently.

How Trump Favored Texas over Puerto Rico (Politico)

Trump: We Cannot Aid Puerto Rico "Forever" (CNN)

Trump Lays Blame on Puerto Ricans for Slow Hurricane Response (Reuters)

On Twitter, Trump Attacks Mayor of San Juan for "Poor Leadership" amid Deepening Crisis (*The Washington Post*)

Donald Trump: Puerto Rico Wants "Everything to Be Done for Them" (*TIME*)

Trump to Puerto Rico: "You've Thrown Our Budget out of Whack" (CNBC)

Trump: Puerto Rico Not "Real Catastrophe like Katrina" (BBC)

While Puerto Rico isn't a US state, it is a US territory. Residents pay some taxes to the US gov—but don't really have any rep in the US gov. Currently, more than ten thousand active-duty military personnel from Puerto Rico serve across the branches of the US Armed Forces. All of which means that it's the federal gov's responsibility to help Puerto Rico in times of trouble just as it would any other part of the US.

Except, as we've just seen above, that's not what happened.

Needless to say, there was a lot of controversy surrounding the back-to-back US gov responses to Hurricane Harvey and Hurricane Maria.

Especially when rebuilding efforts are still—*still*—taking place in Puerto Rico as of this writing.

In fact, the rebuilding is going so slowly that there are concerns that the impact of any future hurricanes could be made that much worse. Hint: almost every building on the island was damaged by Hurricane Maria. Meaning safe, hurricane-proof shelter is pretty much impossible to come by.

So let's take a moment to look back on this section as a whole. Hurricanes are not rare. They occur often. Don't be fooled—this chapter shows just a few key examples of some of the worst hurricanes, but it's certainly not a comprehensive list. Every year when hurricane season sets in, you can bet that there are going to be people whose lives will be destroyed.

That's where we come in.

Maybe we can't control hurricanes (although, heads up—they are getting worse, and more frequent, due to the effects of climate change).

But we do know that, often, the people who are most impacted by them are BIPOC or low income.

And we've already established that money (as in aid) often flows less freely to those groups of people.

So here's what we *can* control: the response. It's up to us to make sure that response isn't dictated by race or nationality or class. And it's also up to us to push for climate action that will help make sure hurricanes aren't getting exponentially more devastating.

Because, yes. Hurricanes do a lot of destruction in the moment.

But there is a big human element to their aftermath, too.

You, me, everyone—we all have the vast potential to do further harm . . . or good.

Your move.

Wildfires

I talked a bit about climate change back in the section on the Movements. I brought that topic up again in connection with hurricanes. And I'm going to talk about it again here, too, because climate change can have some pretty significant effects on wildfires. It's not super complicated: the hotter and drier it is, the better conditions are for wildfires to start and spread.

Let's take a look at what that means with some of the most significant wildfires that have happened recently.

California

I'll start in California.

Let's do another one of those *picture this* kind of things . . .

You wake because you can't breathe.

It's the middle of the night, and you can't breathe, can barely force the air through your nostrils. Every breath feels labored. The air is thick and heavy. You smell something—*smoke*.

You are scared because it is dark.

You're not scared *of* the dark or anything like that. You just know that when you went to bed, the moon was bright and big in the sky. You even thought about getting blinds to block out all that light.

But now? The sky is a deep, dark, orangey red. The world seems as if it's been stained that one single color. If it was a sunset, it'd be breathtakingly beautiful. Now it takes your breath away for a very different reason.

You jump out of bed because of the noise.

It sounds like the earth is being ripped apart. Like great big boulders are rolling down a mountain. Like every tree in the world has suddenly toppled.

The sound grows louder and louder and nearer and nearer until you realize—you *realize*—what is happening.

Fire.

So you stop thinking.

You run from the only room you've ever slept in.

You leave the only house you've ever lived in.

You take absolutely nothing.

You come outside to a world you've never known.

You see countless firefighters helping fight the towering wall of flames, helping people from their beds, helping people flee.

Because that's what you're doing. You're fleeing.

And you don't know when—or if—you'll return.

That's not some apocalyptic scenario. That's something far too many Californians (and really, anyone who's had to experience a wildfire) have faced—some of them, multiple times.

I'm not exaggerating. Not even a little bit.

Here are some of the biggest California fires in recent history:

	Start Date	Time until Contained	Death Toll	Buildings Destroyed	Size
Atlas Fire	10/8/17	20 days	6	781	51,057 acres
Redwood Complex Fire	10/8/17	21 days	9	More than 500	36,523 acres
Tubbs Fire	10/8/17	23 days	22	5,643	36,807 acres
Thomas Fire	12/4/17	About 4 months	2 (plus 21 killed in the aftermath)	1,063	281,893 acres
Carr Fire	7/23/18	Over a month	8	1,604	229,651 acres
Mendocino Complex Fire	7/27/18	More than 3 months	1	280	459,123 acres
Camp Fire	11/8/18	17 days	86	18,804	153,336 acres
SCU Lightning Complex Fires	8/16/20	About a month	0	222	396,624 acres
August Complex Fire	8/16/20	Still not contained	1	935	1,032,648 acres
LNU Lightning Complex Fires	8/17/20	About a month and a half	6	1,491	363,220 acres
North Complex Fire	8/17/20	About four months	16	2,455	318,935 acres
Creek Fire	9/4/20	About four months	0	856	379,895 acres

And these are just the fires that took place between 2017 and 2020. They show a devastating trend: that in recent years, fires have gotten worse and worse, until it seems that it's almost every year that records are being tragically broken. Fires are getting bigger, deadlier, costlier. They're lasting longer. There are more of them.

It's incredibly haunting to realize that aaaaaall this damage, aaaaaall of these deaths . . . occurred in just a few years.

Just four years.

Which begs the question: if and when climate change *really* sets in and it's too late to go back—what will fire season look like?

Will certain areas be made entirely uninhabitable?

Or will millions upon millions of people be doomed to yearly evacuations and the potential loss of their homes—and even their lives?

These questions weigh heavily on the minds of people in California, but that isn't the only place grappling with similar issues. In fact, for a good chunk of 2019, Australia lived that scenario, too.

Australia

Seventy-nine days. That's how long the Australia fires lasted in 2019.

For reference, that's about equal to the amount of school days in a semester.

Now just imagine, for that amount of time: Smoke, everywhere you look, clogging up your throat and your lungs and blotting out the sky. Regular evacuations. The constant threat of losing your home, of your life being taken from you—just like that. And not just your life, but the lives of plants and animals who rely on Australia's diverse ecosystem to survive.

If you've ever had the flu for a week, you know that each one of those days feels like forever. With the Australia fires, it was almost as if most of the country had the flu for months on end, sickening and killing endless life.

Twelve million. That's how many acres were burned in total. Twelve *million*.

If you've ever been to Disneyland, you know how big it is. Twelve million acres is like 142,000 Disneylands, all on fire, for seventy-nine days straight.

Manhattan? Yeah, that's like almost 1,102 Manhattans, all on fire.

Hey, did you know the biggest college campus in the US—Berry College—is 27,000 acres? It would take nearly 445 of those to fill up aaaaall the land that was burned in the Australia fires.

1,000,000,000

That's how many animals were estimated to have died in those fires.

That's like if every pet dog and cat in all of the United States died. Seven times over.

And remember: these fires aren't a new phenomenon, and in small doses they're actually healthy for the environment, because they can clear the way for new growth. But, and this is a big but, they're not supposed to be this big or this bad. And not just that—they're expected to just keep getting worse due to climate change.

Meanwhile, there are other wildfires that occur that don't really have much to do with climate change (although they certainly contribute to it) but definitely still have a human element coming into play. Know what I'm talking about? You guessed it: the Amazon fires.

The Amazon

You might know the Amazon as the lungs of the planet. (Those 2.1 million square acres produce 20 percent of the oxygen in our atmosphere.) You might know the Amazon as the world's largest rainforest. You might know the Amazon as being home to billions of plants and animals.

So, pretty important.

Which made the Amazon fires in 2019 all the more devastating.

If you spend much time on social media, it's super likely you've seen some posts trying to raise awareness about the Amazon fires. But what you may not have known is that these fires weren't caused by anything even remotely natural.

No, these fires were started by people.

When the Amazon fires took place, deforestation (aka clearing large areas of trees) was up 80 percent from the previous year. On top of that, it's important to know that it's common for farmers and ranchers to use fires to clear land and make it ready for use—usually, in a way that's relatively controlled and doesn't get out of hand. But that's not always the case, and it certainly wasn't the case in 2019. Put all those factors together, and what you get is the fact that the Amazon was left burning at the highest rate since 2013.

For context, one and a half soccer fields of rainforest were being destroyed . . . every minute . . . every day.

As the fires set by the farmers spiraled out of control and continued to grow, it became all too clear just how disastrous they were.

Brazil's Amazon Rainforest Suffers Worst Fires in a Decade (*The Guardian*)

Amazon Fires Increase by 84% in One Year— Space Agency (BBC)

Raging Rainforest Fires Darken Skies in Brazil, Inspire #prayforamazonia (NBC News)

Amazon Fires Push the Forest Closer to a Dangerous Tipping Point (PRI.org)

The Amazon Hasn't Stopped Burning. There Were 19,925 Fire Outbreaks Last Month, and 'More Fires' Are in the Future (USA Today)

The Amazon helps give us life. But it's a two-way street.

We can give it life as well, by caring for it and being careful in it. We can give it death just as easily. And the same is true of all of our forests and woodland areas around the world.

Because when it comes to wildfires, a lot less of it is wild than the name actually implies. A good portion of wildfires are started by things like campfires or transformers or deforestation. They're not just some random occurrence. And even if they're not directly caused by people, you've already seen how they're made worse by climate change, which is most definitely a human-made problem.

Through small, individual acts—like properly disposing of hot coals while camping or just generally living a more environmentally conscious life—and big, collective acts—like lobbying for better regulations and voting for officials who recognize the importance of climate change and wildfire prevention—we can play a part in making sure there are fewer wildfires, fewer deaths, fewer homes destroyed each year.

Not more.

Diseases

I'm going to start in the relative present: December 2019. A coronavirus starts to spread in Wuhan, China, making its way to Europe and then the rest of the world.

You probably know everything that happened after that, because you lived it. You lived the months of lockdowns, the months of online school, the months of mask wearing and social distancing and constant caution. The months of watching the death toll climb. The months of waiting with bated breath for a vaccine.

That was a big part of your life—and the lives of the billions of other people on this earth.

But there are whole other sets of people who lived this, too.

Only not in 2019. Not in 2020, or 2021.

They lived it centuries ago, during the time of the plague, of course, but they also lived it much more recently. They lived it in 1918. They lived it between 1916 and 1955. They lived it from 1981 to 1991, too.

Now let's go back to the past.

You've probably heard the 1918 flu pandemic referenced a whole lot during the COVID-19 pandemic.

Medical Historian Compares the Coronavirus to the 1918 Flu Pandemic (CNBC)

How the 1918 and COVID Pandemics Compare (ABC News)

What the 1918 Flu Pandemic Can Teach Us About Coronavirus (CNN)

See?

But despite aaaall the headlines, a pretty big chunk of people don't actually know very much about the 1918 pandemic.

Don't worry. That's where this book comes in.

Let's try something. I'm going to tell you a little bit about that pandemic, and wherever there's a similarity to coronavirus, I'll highlight it.

Sound good?

The 1918 flu first popped up in Europe, the US, and Asia. It wasn't long before it was basically everywhere. And it wasn't long before govs started intro'ing regulations requiring citizens to wear masks and closing down schools, theaters, churches, and bizes.

At the time, there was no drug or vaccine to treat this strain of the flu, which usually affected people one of two ways: by giving them typical flu symptoms, or by killing them just hours or days after they began developing symptoms and experiencing blue skin and fluid-filled lungs. In fact, the 1918 flu was so deadly that it caused the average life expectancy in the US . . . to drop by twelve years.

It probably comes as no surprise that panic broke out around the world.

Hospitals were so overloaded with patients that places like schools and homes were converted into makeshift hospitals. Even then, there was a shortage of workers because so many had either gotten the flu themselves or died during World War I.

Not everyone took the flu so seriously. Some leadership

attributed rising deaths to, you know, the normal flu, rather than the ultradeadly new flu. Instead of locking things down, they went right on with celebrations and parades and all sorts of events.

Until deaths skyrocketed, and people were forced to face the terrifying truth.

It was nearly two years before the pandemic came to an end. The why: everyone who was infected had either died—or developed some sort of immunity. By then, about one-third of the world's population (around five hundred million people) had been sickened and at least fifty million people had died.

Fifty. Million.

Okay. So that's the 1918 flu pandemic—or at least a brief overview of it.

See what I'm getting at yet?

I'll give you another one.

You've probably *also* heard a bit about smallpox, polio, and measles. Hint: it's likely you got shots to prevent you from getting these when you were little. These diseases have been around for a long, long while, but they really hit their peak in the nineteenth and twentieth centuries. Unlike the 1918 flu pandemic or the coronavirus, there wasn't a full-scale lockdown for any of these diseases, so new outbreaks kept popping up until each one became dangerously widespread.

Smallpox Still Prevalent (*The New York Times*, 1891)

U.N. Seeks Smallpox Vaccine (*The New York Times*, 1964)

Global War on Smallpox Expected to Be Won in '76
(*The New York Times*, 1975)

Outbreak of Polio Is Worst Since 1916; Government
Says 5,454 Cases Are Reported in 47 States; Nearly
Double a Year Ago (*The New York Times*, 1946)

24,000 Polio Cases Reported in 1946; This Year's
Epidemic Is Worst in the Country's History, Basil
O'Connor Says (*The New York Times*, 1946)

Nurses Sought for Polio Cases (*The New York Times*, 1952)

Lasting Prevention of Polio Reported in Vaccine Tests
(*The New York Times*, 1954)

Measles Vaccine Effective in Test; Injections with Live
Virus Protect 100 Per Cent of Children in Epidemics; May
Be Ready in 1962; Gamma Globulin Is Utilized to Reduce
Reactions of Earlier Experiments (*The New York Times*, 1961)

2 Measles Vaccines Licensed; U.S. Sees End of Disease
in 1965; U.S. Authorizes 2 Measles Drugs; Vaccine
Actions Differ (*The New York Times*, 1963)

Also unlike the 1918 pandemic (though thankfully, much like the coronavirus one), this time around, there *were* vaccines eventually developed for measles, polio, and smallpox. This pretty much changed the game around all diseases, especially epidemic ones (liiiiike COVID-19). Forever. Now there was the ability to develop protection against diseases beyond any other the human race had had before.

It was, quite literally, a lifesaver.

But even with the possibility of vaccines, this wasn't the last the world would see of epidemics. And before you go *Well, duh*, no, we're not talking about coronavirus. Yet.

AIDS (acquired immunodeficiency syndrome) is a condition that can result from HIV (human immunodeficiency virus). Aka a virus that attacks the immune system. It's transmitted through certain bodily fluids, and it's extra dangerous because it eliminates the body's ability to fight infections and diseases. If you have AIDS and you get cancer or something like pneumonia, there's little hope of survival. Think: colds can easily become pneumonia, cancers that would otherwise be defeated by the immune system (which, FYI, a lot of cancers are) take hold . . .

The reigning theory is that HIV—and, thus, AIDS—probably came from chimpanzees who were infected with almost the same virus. It made the leap from animal to human when hunters in Africa ate infected chimpanzees or the blood of these chimpanzees somehow got into the hunters' injuries.

Over time, HIV spread around the world. But it wasn't until 1981 when people started hearing about AIDS.

This is a good place to mention how this all ties in with LGBTQ+ rights. Because when AIDS began appearing in American society, most of those who were infected were gay men. It all came down to how the disease was most easily transmitted.

That led to the disease's original name: GRID.

Gay-related immune deficiency.

That wasn't some public nickname; no, that's literally what officials called it. People also called it things like the "gay plague."

And not everyone was all that upset about it.

At least not at first.

Case in point: as you read in the LGBTQ+ Rights Movement

chapter, 1981 is right around when the advancements for LGBTQ+ rights ground to a halt and figures like Anita Bryant began gaining popularity. Cries for medical help from the LGBTQ+ community . . . went largely unanswered.

And those cries for help were very, very dire. By the end of 1981, there were 270 reported cases of what was later discovered to be AIDS. 121 of the people who had it died. People were frightened beyond belief. They didn't quite understand what was going on, and even worse, no one was doing much to find a solution. If you were diagnosed with AIDS, it was pretty much seen as a death sentence. People—young people—would go in to the doctor and leave carrying the knowledge they had just a couple years or even months left to live.

Prez Ronald Reagan didn't ever mention the word "AIDS" publicly until 1985, after twelve thousand Americans had already died of the disease. Gov officials were even recorded laughing and making jokes about the epidemic.

Fast-forward to 1987, and the first drug to treat AIDS came out. But it didn't go so far as to prevent death, and the dosage patients were told to take actually equated to toxic overdose.

So LGBTQ+ activists took it upon themselves to fix things with an "inside-outside" strategy.

At first, they did things like offer care to AIDS patients. They helped bring people to the hospital. They worked to provide comfort to those who were sick and dying. They connected patients with lawyers to write their wills (that's how little hope there was for survival).

But those initial actions began expanding as anger over the gov's inaction grew. People were absolutely furious that the gov literally did not seem to care about their lives. And it wasn't just the gov—the general public, the scientific community . . . no one was helping.

Enter: Protests. Marches. Rallies. Lobbying. Die-ins (a demonstration in which people lie down in a particular place as if they're dead). Shutting down interstates. Activist groups like AIDS Coalition

to Unleash Power (aka ACT UP), which was founded to push the gov
and the scientific community to get their act together and start
saving lives.

It worked. The gov listened and got to work on treatments.

By 1995, AIDS was the greatest killer of men ages twenty-five
to forty-four in all of the United States. And millions of people were
being infected around the world, too.

The same year, the gov greenlighted the first protease inhibitors,
which were a type of drug that could put an end to and even reverse
the progression of AIDS when combined with some other treatments.

But problems persisted.

The drug was highly expensive, which turned AIDS into not just
an issue of health and LGBTQ+ rights, but also one of money. Only
the rich could be saved.

And saved they were. The next year, the number of deaths plum-
meted for the first time ever. What else made records: the fact that
Black people were now being diagnosed with AIDS more frequently
than white people.

So fast-forward to 2003, and Prez George W. Bush gave the thumbs-up to a program that buys and distributes lifesaving HIV medications to people all over the world who couldn't otherwise afford them. It became the largest-ever gov program fighting a single disease. And while it didn't solve the problem entirely—people are still HIV positive today, since these lifesaving medications aren't cures, they're just very, very effective treatments; and because some people still don't have access to treatment—it totally changed the course of the disease. And showed us the power not only of our gov to step up and save lives, but of individual citizens to step up and push for change.

Let's take a step back and sum things up for all of these disasters. There's been one running theme across pretty much all of them, and that is that they aren't always human-made, but they always affect humans. And usually, the humans being affected fall into a very specific group of people: The disenfranchised. The underprivileged.

These disasters don't create the issues of inequity, of course. But they exacerbate them. They bring them out into the open where everyone can see them and make it really, really hard to look away.

Then they wait and see what we do.

Cramm This Conclusion

Okay. So you've just read this book. (Go you.) In doing so, you've learned about the issues, the connections, the history behind so many of the things that happen in the now. You've done that work—or at least you've started to—and you've gotten a good look at the problems out there. And, yeah. There are a lot of them.

What next?

Whenever you see a problem in life, whether small and local or large and global, you always have two choices: see the problem and ignore it, or see the problem and go fix the thing.

You get to pick.

But it's also important to keep in mind that a good portion of the world doesn't get to just *see* the problem. A good portion of the world wakes up every day and faces at least one of these problems rather than, say, reading about it in a book. Maybe you're one of those people. Maybe you're not. And in the latter case, I'll make it extra clear: even if you don't know that you're making a decision as to whether or not to get involved, you always are. It's a choice and a privilege to hear about a problem rather than live the problem. And it's a choice and a privilege to go on living as if the problem never existed in the first place.

Plenty of people pick that option. And that right there? That's yet another problem.

But maybe we can change that. And by *we*, I mean you and me and everyone else reading this. I mean our generation. I mean the tweens and the teens and the twentysomethings. The first-time voters and the organizers and the social media activists and beyond.

Maybe we can delve deeper.

Maybe we can go back and figure out where these problems started and how they've continued to hurt people throughout history.

Maybe we can follow the breadcrumbs all the way to the present and realize just how deeply rooted these problems are.

Maybe we can start to dig way down in the dirt and grab those roots and just *yank* them out of the ground. Maybe we can plant new seeds, new roots, but this time, ones built on ideas of hope and equity and justice. This time, ones built on ideas of progress and community and the desire to do good.

I believe we can. Otherwise, I wouldn't have written this book at all.

But I did write this book. And now I'm giving you a choice. It's the same choice everyone has had throughout all of time. It's the same choice you watched people make throughout this book, either leading to more hatred, more cruelty—or to more good.

Gen Z is just getting started. Think of all the change we've made in a few short years. We've proven time and time again that we don't need years of experience under our belts. We just need a cause. A voice. A fresh outlook. A purpose. And some knowledge to back it all up.

And when we have those things? There's nothing we can't do.

You've read about the context and the background to a bunch of the problems facing us today. You know where the issues lie and where things stand now.

Now what?

The world awaits your answer.

Sources

Alberta Civil Liberties Research Centre. "Forms of Racism." Accessed July 15, 2020. aclrc.com/forms-of-racism.

Almasy, Steve. "March for Our Lives: Top Moments That Made Up a Movement." CNN. March 25, 2018. cnn.com/2018/03/24/us/march-for-our-lives-wrap/index .html.

American Defamation League. "Antisemitism." Accessed July 18, 2020. adl.org /anti-semitism.

Ankel, Sophia. "30 Days that Shook America: Since the Death of George Floyd, the Black Lives Matter Movement Has Already Changed the Country." Business Insider, June 24, 2020. businessinsider.com/13-concrete-changes-sparked-by -george-floyd-protests-so-far-2020-6.

Bakali, Naved. "Islamophobia and the Law: Unpacking Structural Islamophobia." Yaqeen Institute for Islamic Research, November 14, 2019. yaqeeninstitute.org /navedbakali/islamophobia-and-the-law-unpacking-structural-islamophobia.

Bates, Karen Grigsby. "A Look Back at Trayvon Martin's Death, and the Movement It Inspired." NPR, July 31, 2018. npr.org/sections/codeswitch/2018/07/31 /631897758/a-look-back-at-trayvon-martins-death-and-the-movement-it -inspired.

Boyle, Michael J. "The Great Recession." Investopedia. Last modified October 23, 2020. investopedia.com/terms/g/great-recession.asp.

Bryan, Wright, and Douglas Hopper. "Iraq WMD Timeline: How the Mystery Unraveled." NPR. November 15, 2005. npr.org/templates/story/story .php?storyId=4996218.

Centers for Disease Control and Prevention. "1918 Pandemic." Last modified March 20, 2019. cdc.gov/flu/pandemic-resources/1918-pandemic-h1n1.html.

The Editors of Encyclopedia Britannica. "Afghanistan War." Britannica. Last modified November 14, 2018. britannica.com/event/Afghanistan-War.

The Editors of Encyclopedia Britannica. "Arab Spring." Britannica. Last modified January 27, 2021. britannica.com/event/Arab-Spring.

The Editors of Encyclopedia Britannica. "Balfour Declaration." Britannica. Last modified October 26, 2020. britannica.com/event/Balfour-Declaration.

The Editors of Encyclopedia Britannica. "Cold War." Britannica. Last modified September 17, 2020. britannica.com/event/Cold-War.

The Editors of Encyclopedia Britannica. "Egypt Uprising of 2011." Britannica. Last modified January 18, 2021. britannica.com/event/Egypt-Uprising-of-2011.

The Editors of Encyclopedia Britannica. "Hippie." Britannica. Last modified May 22, 2020. britannica.com/topic/hippie.

The Editors of Encyclopedia Britannica. "Hurricane Katrina." Britannica. Last modified September 23, 2020. britannica.com/event/Hurricane-Katrina.

The Editors of Encyclopedia Britannica. "Iraq War." Britannica. Last modified November 4, 2020. britannica.com/event/Iraq-War.

The Editors of Encyclopedia Britannica. "Jasmine Revolution." Britannica. Last modified January 21, 2021. britannica.com/event/Jasmine-Revolution.

The Editors of Encyclopedia Britannica. "Revolution Day." Britannica. Last modified July 22, 2020. britannica.com/topic/Revolution-Day.

Eisenmenger, Ashley. "Ableism 101: What It Is, What It Looks Like, and What We Can Do to Fix It." Access Living, December 12, 2019. accessliving.org/newsroom/blog/ableism-101.

Gallup. "Islamophobia: Understanding Anti-Muslim Sentiment in the West." Accessed July 18, 2020. https://news.gallup.com/poll/157082/islamophobia-understanding-anti-muslim-sentiment-west.aspx.

Greenspan, Jesse. "The Rise and Fall of Smallpox." History. Last modified May 15, 2020. history.com/news/the-rise-and-fall-of-smallpox.

Griggs, Brandon. "Hiding under a Desk as a Gunman Roamed the Halls, a Terrified Student Live-Tweeted a School Shooting." CNN, February 15, 2018. cnn.com/2018/02/15/us/student-live-tweeting-florida-school-shooting-trnd/index.html.

History.com Editors. "Al Qaeda." History. Last modified September 9, 2019. history.com/topics/21st-century/al-qaeda.

History.com Editors. "Civil Rights Act of 1964." History. Last modified January 25, 2021. history.com/topics/black-history/civil-rights-act.

History.com Editors. "Congress Passes the 19th Amendment, Giving Women the Right to Vote." History. Last modified June 3, 2020. history.com/this-day-in-history/congress-passes-the-19th-amendment.

History.com Editors. "Ho Chi Minh." History. Last modified March 30, 2020. history.com/topics/vietnam-war/ho-chi-minh-1.

History.com Editors. "India and Pakistan Win Independence." History. Last modified August 12, 2020. history.com/this-day-in-history/india-and-pakistan-win-independence.

History.com Editors. "Korean War." History. Last modified May 11, 2020. history.com/topics/korea/korean-war.

History.com Editors. "Nuclear Disaster at Three Mile Island." History. Last modified March 25, 2020. history.com/this-day-in-history/nuclear-accident-at-three-mile-island.

History.com Editors. "State of Israel Proclaimed." History. Last modified May 12, 2020. history.com/this-day-in-history/state-of-israel-proclaimed.

History.com Editors. "Vietnam War." History. Last modified August 19, 2020. history.com/topics/vietnam-war/vietnam-war-history.

Islamophobia101.com. "Islamophobia 101." Last modified May 13, 2019. islamophobia.org/research/islamophobia-101.html.

Langone, Alix. "#MeToo and Time's Up Founders Explain the Difference Between the 2 Movements—and How They're Alike." *TIME*. March 8, 2018. https://time. com/5189945/whats-the-difference-between-the-metoo-and-times-up -movements.

Musho, Lee. "The March: Minute by Minute." NewsHouse, January 22, 2019. thenewshouse.com/off-campus/a-timeline-for-the-march-for-our-lives.

LGBTQ History. "LGBTQ Rights Timeline in American History." Accessed July 17, 2020. lgbtqhistory.org/lgbt-rights-timeline-in-american-history.

NASA. "Global Climate Change." Accessed July 10, 2020. https://climate.nasa.gov.

Oxford Languages and Google. "English Dictionary." Accessed January 11, 2021. https://languages.oup.com/google-dictionary-en/

Pallardy, Richard. "Deepwater Horizon Oil Spill." Britannica. Last modified November 2, 2020. britannica.com/event/Deepwater-Horizon-oil-spill.

Pells, Richard H. "Great Depression." Britannica. Last modified September 10, 2020. britannica.com/event/Great-Depression.

Pruitt, Sarah. "How the Vietnam War Empowered the Hippie Movement." History. Last modified March 18, 2019. history.com/news/vietnam-war-hippies-counter -culture.

Pruitt, Sarah. "Why Are North and South Korea Divided?" History. Last modified January 15, 2019. history.com/news/north-south-korea-divided-reasons-facts.

Purdue, A. W. "The Transformative Impact of World War II." EGO: European History Online. Last modified April 18, 2016. http://ieg-ego.eu/en/threads /alliances-and-wars/war-as-an-agent-of-transfer/a-w-purdue-the -transformative-impact-of-world-war-ii.

"Race an Issue in Katrina Response." CBS News, September 3, 2005. cbsnews.com /news/race-an-issue-in-katrina-response.

Rafferty, John P. "9 of the Biggest Oil Spills in History." Britannica. Accessed June 18, 2020. britannica.com/list/9-of-the-biggest-oil-spills-in-history.

Robinson, Kali. "The Arab Spring at Ten Years: What's the Legacy of the Uprisings?" Council on Foreign Relations, December 3, 2020. cfr.org/article/arab-spring -ten-years-whats-legacy-uprisings.

Rogers, Kara. "AIDS." Britannica. Last modified October 1, 2020. britannica.com /science/AIDS.

Rosen, Rebecca J. "So, Was Facebook Responsible for the Arab Spring After All?" *The Atlantic*, September 3, 2011. theatlantic.com/technology/archive/2011/09/so -was-facebook-responsible-for-the-arab-spring-after-all/244314.

Spector, Ronald H. "The Vietnam War and the Media." Britannica. Last modified April 27, 2016. britannica.com/topic/The-Vietnam-War-and-the-media-2051426.

United Nations. "The Struggle to Help Hurricane-Hit Caribbean Continues, UN Relief Wing Says." UN News. September 8, 2008. https://news.un.org/en /story/2008/09/272162-struggle-help-hurricane-hit-caribbean-continues -un-relief-wing-says.

United States Institute of Peace. "Egypt Timeline: Since the Arab Uprising." Last modified July 2, 2019. usip.org/egypt-timeline-arab-uprising.

Weinstein, Adam, and the MoJo News Team. "The Trayvon Martin Killing,

Explained." *Mother Jones*, March 18, 2012. motherjones.com/politics/2012/03 /what-happened-trayvon-martin-explained.

"What Are the Proposed Solutions to the Israeli-Palestinian Conflict?" Accessed July 21, 2020. Alma. heyalma.com/israel-guide/what-are-the-proposed -solutions-to-the-israeli-palestinian-conflict.

Witt, Emily. "How the Survivors of Parkland Began the Never Again Movement." *The New Yorker*, February 19, 2018. newyorker.com/news/news-desk/how-the -survivors-of-parkland-began-the-never-again-movement.

World Bank. "Rapidly Assessing the Impact of Hurricane Matthew in Haiti." Last modified October 20, 2017. worldbank.org/en/results/2017/10/20/rapidly -assessing-the-impact-of-hurricane-matthew-in-haiti.

Photo Credits

Page 56, Wikimedia Commons/Bundesarchiv, B 145 Bild-P091010 / CC-BY-SA 3.0; Page 60, Wikimedia Commons; Page 66, Wikimedia Commons (all); Page 68, Wikimedia Commons; Page 70, Wikimedia Commons (all); Page 81, Wikimedia Commons; Page 83, Wikimedia Commons/Justin McIntosh; Page 85, Wikimedia Commons/Israel Defense Forces; Page 97, Wikimedia Commons; Page 100, Wikimedia Commons; Page 109, Wikimedia Commons; Page 121, Wikimedia Commons; Page 124, Wikimedia Commons; Page 127, Wikimedia Commons (all); Page 129, National Archives; Page 131, Wikimedia Commons; Page 132, Wikimedia Commons/National Archive (top left), Wikimedia Commons/UW Digital Collections (top right), Wikimedia Commons (bottom); Page 133, Wikimedia Commons/Derek Redmond and Paul Campbell; Page 137, Wikimedia Commons; Page 140, Wikimedia Commons; Page 141, Wikimedia Commons; Page 142, Wikimedia Commons/Adam Jones; Page 143, Wikimedia Commons (all); Page 145, Wikimedia Commons; Page 146, Library of Congress; Page 147, Wikimedia Commons (all); Page 158, Wikimedia Commons/Daniel Nicoletta; Page 165, Wikimedia Commons/AlMahras; Page 166, Wikimedia Commons/Magharebia; Page 172, Wikimedia Commons (all); Page 175, Wikimedia Commons/Debra Sweet; Page 176, Wikimedia Commons/ann harkness; Page 181, Wikimedia Commons; Page 189, Wikimedia Commons/Rhododendrites (all); Page 197, Wikimedia Commons/ Ted Eytan (top left), Wikimedia Commons/Gregory Varnum (top right), Wikimedia Commons/Tristan Loper (bottom left), Wikimedia Commons/Fibonacci Blue (bottom right); Page 203, Wikimedia Commons/Anders Hellberg; Page 204, Wikimedia Commons/Frankie Fouganthin; Page 205, Wikimedia Commons/Tiziana Rigodanzo; Page 211, Wikimedia Commons (top), Wikimedia Commons (bottom left), Wikimedia Commons/kris krüg (bottom right); Page 213, Wikimedia Commons; Page 217, Wikimedia Commons/IAEA Imagebank; Page 219, Wikimedia Commons/IAEA Imagebank; Page 221, Wikimedia Commons/IAEA Imagebank; Page 223, Wikimedia Commons; Page 224, Wikimedia Commons (all); Page 230, Wikimedia Commons (top), Wikimedia Commons (bottom left), Wikimedia Commons/Daniel Lobo (bottom right); Page 232, Wikimedia Commons (all); Page 233, Wikimedia Commons/ Coralie Giese, CDC; Page 234, Wikimedia Commons/Master Sgt. Mark C. Olsen/U.S. Air Force/New Jersey National Guard; Page 235, Wikimedia Commons/2C2K Photography; Page 236, Wikimedia Commons; Page 240, Wikimedia Commons; Page 242, Wikimedia Commons (all); Page 252, Wikimedia Commons

Acknowledgments

I don't think there are enough words in the dictionary to properly thank Talia Benamy, my editor. You were the first person who's not my parent to ever edit my writing. I will forever be grateful to you for taking a chance on a sixteen-year-old girl. I have this vivid memory of our first call together: you said something about the book and I nearly leapt out of my seat and exclaimed, "It's like you're pulling words right out of my head!" The entire process of working on this book with you has felt like that moment, over and over again.

To Seth Fishman, my literary agent, thank you for your genuine excitement for this project from the very start. I truly couldn't imagine there being a better agent. I'm endlessly appreciative of all your answers to my many questions about the book world. You made what could have been an overwhelming first step into publishing one of the best experiences of my life. My childhood dream was always to become a published author, and thanks to you, I've gotten to accomplish that dream earlier than I ever expected. Thank you also to everyone else at the Gernert Company for all you've done for me.

Justin Weber and Jon Huddle, thank you for supporting my work with The Cramm and for being the first to encourage me to pursue writing this book.

A massive thank you to all the fantastic people at Philomel Books, especially Krista Ahlberg, Madeleine Vasaly, Monique Sterling, and Kristie Radwilowicz.

Thank you to Eden Andrulaitis, who's responsible for all the incredible illustrations in this book, for dedicating so much of your time to helping make this project come alive. It's been an honor to work with you, and I can't wait to see where your talents take you in the future.

I am indebted to the countless experts, journalists, professors, and researchers who graciously took the time to read over this book and offer notes, feedback, and resources. This project would not be what it is without your help.

Thank you to everyone who let me use your tweets and posts in this book, including Eric Griggs, Kelynn Carter Poinsette, Patrisse Cullors, Preston Mitchum, and Uneak Tershai.

To my mom, my dad, Oscar, and Tuesday, thank you a million times over for making me so profoundly overjoyed to wake up each day just so I can spend more time with you all. You're my favorite people (and poodle) on this planet. I don't know how I got lucky enough to have you all as my family. Thank you especially to my parents for telling me, even as a young girl, that I didn't need to wait until I was older to start chasing after my dreams. When I was eight and decided I wanted to learn how to build websites, you helped find me a program to do so. When I was eleven and decided I wanted to write a fantasy novel, you spent time helping me create an outline, brainstorm ideas, and edit my writing. And when I was twelve and decided I wanted to start a news organization for my generation, you never once doubted that I was capable (or got annoyed with me for accidentally waking you up at five a.m. while writing). Oscar, thank you for your brilliance and your humor. And Tuesday, thank you for always lifting my spirits.

Thank you to Brandee Barker and Kenny Van Zant for your belief in The Cramm and your guidance. It's such an honor to work with you and learn from you. Thank you also to Callie Schweitzer for our many enlightening conversations.

To Andy, Arunima, Christopher, Joshua, Michelle, and Shaan (aka the global babygirls), thank you for being my second family. I will never stop being amazed that we've all managed to find each other from our respective corners of the earth. See you in New York (or Johannesburg, or Quebec, or Paris).

Aqsa, Jade, and Maryam, thank you for taking the time to read over my final(ish) draft of the book and give such thoughtful and helpful notes. Your perspective was invaluable.

Thank you to Maddie, Elise, and Randy for being there for me since what feels like birth. I know I tell you this every time I see you, but I'm beyond grateful to you for your continuous support. To Maddie in particular, thank you for being the sister I never had.

To my wonderful friends Peyton, Kathryn, and Gracie, thank you for sticking with me over the years. I have so much love for you all.

Thank you to everyone at *Teen Vogue*, *The Today Show*, NPR, *Forbes*, *The Economist*, *The New York Times Upfront*, In The Know, *Barron's*, *WIRED*, *Grazia*, UNICEF, Jewish Telegraphic Agency, Süddeutsche Zeitung, and more who've covered The Cramm and helped bring us exposure. Thank you especially to Rainesford Stauffer, who gave The Cramm our first big press and opened more doors than you know.

A big thank you to The Cramm Fam—our Editorial Team, Media Team, Organizing Team, and Social Media Team members and everyone else who's part of the fam—for deciding you believed in The Cramm's mission enough to spend your time helping out. I'll always be in awe of that.

And to everyone who's ever read, followed, watched, listened to, or supported The Cramm, thank you for quite literally everything. You're the reason this book happened. Thank you, thank you, thank you.